To Sallie
from
Mom & Dad
Dec. 25, 1972

The Rainbow Book of Nature

THE RAINBOW BOOK OF
NATURE

By Donald Culross Peattie

ILLUSTRATED BY RUDOLF FREUND

WORLD PUBLISHING
TIMES MIRROR
NEW YORK

PUBLISHED BY THE WORLD PUBLISHING COMPANY

PUBLISHED SIMULTANEOUSLY IN CANADA

BY NELSON, FOSTER & SCOTT LTD.

1972 PRINTING

LIBRARY OF CONGRESS CATALOG CARD NUMBER: 57–5896

ISBN 0–529–04615–6 (TRADE EDITION)

ISBN 0–529–04673–3 (LIBRARY EDITION)

PRINTED IN THE UNITED STATES OF AMERICA

WORLD PUBLISHING
TIMES MIRROR

CONTENTS

III. The Colors of Life

IV. The Forms of Life

V. Hours and Seasons

I.

"THE WORLD IS SO FULL..."

COME OUT AND LOOK!

ID you ever wake up early and slip out into a world fresh with a new day? The familiar scene sparkles with beauty and wonder and the sense of possible adventure. The air smells, perhaps, of pine needles and wood smoke and a secret, earthy odor like mushrooms. The grass is alight with dewdrops darting tiny rainbow fires. There may be squirrels playing tag in the trees, tweaking each other's tails, behaving as if life were one long frolic. Or crows are telegraphing in their ragged code all the gossip of the sunburnt clearings, the far-off groves. The ants in their dusty hill at your feet are toiling, the workers slavishly hurrying to and fro, the soldiers patrolling stiffly. On a branch a black and yellow spider works out in glittering silk the perfect geometry of her web. And through the aspens runs a panic whispering, as if the trees leaned together to tell old tales of Indian scares and forest dangers.

How did it all come to be here, this shining, quivering, intensely alive world of Nature? Is that only an empty cawing, or have the crows a real language? How does the spider know how to spin her complicated web? How are the ants communicating with one another? Why do the aspen leaves turn like that, with a rustle and patter and twinkle, when the breeze is too faint to stir the leaves of other trees?

Every question is a path inviting you into the adventure of the morning. As soon as you start off on such questions, you are beginning to be a naturalist. And when you begin to find out the answers, the world of Nature takes on a new dimension, as though you had put on glasses which gave depth where everything was flat before, and sharpened all to sudden clarity.

For curiosity is the beginning of natural history—which has no end. The history of Nature, the study of living things, is too vast a subject to get between the covers of a book like this. We couldn't begin to open up, let alone answer, all the questions that will occur to you just from looking at the pictures. And many questions have no answer—yet. Many common happenings are mysterious still, like the migration of birds, or the return of salmon from the sea to their breeding grounds up-river. The science of natural history is never through with its work; it is an endless journey of discovery that is taken up, and carried a little farther, by each generation. The generations come and go. The wonder and beauty of Nature remain.

This life of ours, which is shared by the crows and the squirrels, the ants and the spiders, is itself the most profound of all the mysteries. Where it began, no one can say, and where it goes to, not

the wisest knows. We only feel it, warm and secret in our blood; we see it in the racing of a dog across the grass, hear it in the whistle of a bird, know it as a God-sent gift to be cared for as sacred, whether in ourselves or others. Life, like the morning light streaming down from the sun, fills the world with color and warmth and delight. It is when the tiny prism of the dewdrop catches the sunshine that we can see the rainbow tints in it. So in a book like this we can only catch glimpses of the glittering great whole of Nature.

The study of life is called biology, and much of it is done in laboratories by trained scientists. But the happy, out-of-doors side of the same study is natural history. And anyone can pursue it, and make some good catches too. Just going fishing is apt to be a lesson in natural history, and so is raising racing pigeons or making a butterfly collection or even going to the zoo. Sharp eyes, an inquiring mind, and a good memory are the only laboratory equipment you need. Young people have a finer set of such tools than the most learned oldsters.

In ornithology (the science of birds) the case is well known of an eleven-year-old girl who could name every kind of duck, as far off as she could see it, by the way it flew. Most duck-hunters, grown men, will tell you that it takes years of experience to master the difficult subject of the ducks. But since no one remembered

to tell this girl how hard it was, she found it quite easy. She had good eyes, close attention, and a memory that kept what it caught. And these are much more useful than the costliest binoculars ever made.

Not long ago there was a boy who went fishing, and "never got a bite." Yet he came home with the biggest bite you ever saw—the jawbone of a mastodon, an extinct kind of elephant! He had uncovered it in the bank of a stream. He drew a picture of it, explaining his find, and sent it to a natural history museum in Buffalo. The very next day brought some of the museum scientists down to his home town. And when they uncovered the rest of the mastodon skeleton, they found it was an entirely new kind—or, as the scientists say, a new species.

Not all of us can discover a species new to science. But if a thing is new to you or me, it is as good as new. Nor can anybody ever come to the end of discovery. "The world is so full of a number of things," says the cheerful verse, "I'm sure we should all be as happy as kings."

Just what is that number—the number of living things in this world? The number of *kinds* of living things, that is, of species?

It's a good question, but not an easy one. It can't be answered exactly. Naturalists have not finished the count; they are still exploring the world, finding new species in the depths of the sea, in the tropical jungles, even right around us in the thickly settled parts of the globe. Therefore we can give only a rough estimate. It makes a grandly simple sum:

About 700,000 species of animals known
About 300,000 species of plants known
The total is: About 1,000,000 species of known living things

One million species, each with its own name, size, shape, color, habits, range! Who could master so much knowledge? Nobody, of course, not the cleverest student in the world, not in a hundred years. No wonder that the science of natural history is carried on by specialists, who limit themselves each to his own field of interest. The older such a scientist grows, the more he knows about less and less! But you and I are free as the morning to learn only for fun. And learning is a gate that swings wide open, into the out-of-doors, where you will find yourself happy and at home in Nature for all your life long.

WILDERNESS WEALTH

No one was ever more at home in Nature than the American Indian in the days before the first white men came to our shores. Then this great land of ours was all one glorious wilderness, stretching unfenced, unmapped, unspoiled, from ocean to ocean. Never in the history of mankind was there such an abundance of natural life. Mighty forests covered the country from the Atlantic Coast to the beginning of the great plains. The roots of those trees sank deep in black loam rich with the fallen leaves of uncounted centuries. In their lofty branches flocked gaudy, raucous parakeets and shimmering passenger pigeons—birds that no longer exist anywhere on earth today. Through the green forest silence stalked elk and deer and moose. Bear and cougar, mink and fox prowled there. Out on the prairies

18

the bison roamed in vast herds. The biggest of all our animals, the bison or buffalo, numbered in those days as many as fifty million, and the earth shook to the thunder of their hooves when they galloped across the wide free prairie.

Of all this the Indian was part, as no man has been since. He was, as an observer, the world's best naturalist. For the Indian boy, instead of going to school, was trained from earliest childhood to know the wilderness about him. His life depended upon such skill. So he learned to move on his moccasined feet through the forest without cracking a twig or scuffling a leaf. He could paddle his canoe without taking the paddle out of the water or making a

ripple big enough to be heard by even a listening sentinel beaver.

Sometimes, in the days before he got horses from the white men, he hunted the buffalo by imitating a deer. He crept through the tall prairie grass, wearing on his head a deer's head with antlers. He had studied the deer so closely that he could exactly copy the gait of one idly grazing and the jerky way it sometimes moved its head in walking. Buffalo, of course, were not afraid of deer, and allowed them to crop freely near the herd. Thus the red hunters deceived the great beasts till they were near enough to send an arrow or lance speeding into some vital part.

These master hunters studied every sound in the listening world around them. They could imitate the bleating of a fawn by blowing on a little whistle made out of the stems of reed grass. The mother does would thus be lured by the false fawn's cries till they came close to the crouching redskin waiting to bring them down. Or, with a horn of birch bark, Indians mimicked the blatting of the moose cows and so called the bull moose to their ambush. When he set his trap for beaver, the Indian baited it with aspen poles because he knew that the bark of the aspen is the beaver's favorite food.

Yet though they hunted so constantly and skillfully, the Indians did not really destroy any part of that rich, pure wilderness. They hunted, just as the animals themselves did, only to fill their needs at the time. They were true sportsmen, for they pitted their craft fairly against the animal's own. And they did not kill for idle fun, but only to feed hunger.

It was the white men, the pioneers, who began the destruction of America's primeval wilderness. When they came to "settle up" the country, the passenger pigeons were so many that they actually broke with their weight the branches of the giant beech trees. On the nuts of these beeches they loved to feast. But the pioneers, needing clearings and logs to build houses there, cut down these

forests. They slaughtered the pigeons in great quantities, far more
than they could eat in pigeon pies, and turned the pigs in to feed
on them. They killed the buffalo on the prairies in the same need-
less, heedless way. Millions of those giants with shaggy bearded
heads and curving horns were finished off in just a few years.
Travelers crossing the plains even shot them for fun from the train
windows! No wonder that the Plains Indians were filled with grief
and fury to see their fine wild cattle killed so senselessly.

For the red man felt himself very much a part of the animal
kingdom. Often he pitied the beasts he had to kill in order to get
food, clothing, blankets, shelter. He believed, sometimes, that different Indian families were descended from some Super-Animal,
back in the first days of creation. Thus an Indian might belong
to the bear clan or the wolf clan or the frog clan, turtle clan, raven

clan, or coyote clan. We smile at such ideas, but there was a grain of goodness and truth in them.

For it is good, surely, to feel kinship with the animals. Many of our deepest feelings are shared by the beasts, both tame and wild. We have all seen frightened animals, angry animals, animals in pain, or tired, or curious. They can show great loyalty and love, and a touching tenderness to their young. And, like us, they all come helpless into this world, and in the end they too have to leave it. When that time comes, you can read the sadness in their eyes as they say farewell to life.

And, seeing that look, a thoughtful human knows that he too is a part of Nature as the red man was in the days when wilderness was young. True that we are not so at home in the wild as he was. Instead, we have mastered the natural world in our own way. That this way meant much of its destruction is a sorrowful thing to all who love forest depths and secret swamps, free-running beasts, and bird song. But it is a tragedy which had to happen. Without it, we could not have today this powerful, crowding nation rising on American soil.

There is still left, all about us, much natural life to enjoy and cherish. It is gentler now but no less full of fascination and delight. And it finds its own way—sly and shy, bold or wary—right into the heart of our great stone cities.

CITY SECRETS

THE towers of New York City rise glittering into the sky, the tallest of them, the Empire State Building, over a thousand feet high. On a clear day you can see fifty miles from its windy top. But one night it was wrapped in dense fog. And a great flock of little sky-travelers, birds winging southward on their autumn migration, smacked right into it. Next morning people on the street were horrified to find hundreds of jewel-bright warblers lying dead at the foot of the highest building in the world.

Even in daytime many birds are killed on our skyscrapers. Their big windows reflect the sky and clouds, the safe, free air, so that

25

a bird may dash unaware against the glass, and break its delicate neck.

But the city is not always a trap and a danger to wild things. Sometimes they become quite at home in it, finding that it fits certain of their needs excellently. Away down at the most crowded tip of Manhattan Island, in Wall Street, the heart of the financial district, there are falcons hunting. Known in Europe as the peregrine falcon, also called duck hawk here in America, this is the famous bird of prey that kings and princes throughout history have used as a hunting bird. It can be trained to sit on the wrist of the falconer, and when small game birds are seen, the bird is tossed in the air and sent off in pursuit of them. Mounting above its prey, the peregrine then closes its wings and dive-bombs at speeds as much as a hundred and fifty to two hundred miles an hour! No dove or pigeon or duck can fly fast enough to escape the peregrine. And a trained falcon will bring the captured game bird back to its master.

This fierce-eyed hunter likes to nest on the ledge of some lofty cliff where its young will be safe and where it can scan the air below for passing prey. What could be better than the ledges of the cliff-like skyscraper walls? One nest of duck hawks was found behind the electric sign on top of the fashionable St. Regis Hotel. Another pair decided to live in the crannies of the Gothic tower of the Riverside Church. The soaring pinnacle of the Chrysler Building appealed to another duck hawk couple, and the George Washington Bridge makes an ideal site for falcons to harry the ducks far below on the Hudson.

The downtown streets are happy hunting grounds, full of the falcon's favorite prey—pigeons. In the thickest traffic you'll see these city-lovers go strutting on their coral-pink feet, throatily cooing, puffing out their soft mother-of-pearl-colored breasts. They, and their close relatives, the homing and various other breeds of fancy pigeons, are all descended from the same wild bird, the blue rock dove of Europe and Asia. Ancient records show that pigeons were domesticated by the Egyptians as far back as 3000 B.C. A system of pigeon-post—letter-carrying by pigeons—was established by the Sultan of Bagdad in 1150 A.D. For centuries pigeons have been protected in the great square in front of St. Mark's cathedral in Venice. Street vendors sell little cones of grain to passers-by who feed the pigeons all day long, and so tame have they become they light on your head and shoulders and feed from your hands. But when the great bells ring from the tower, they swirl up by the hundreds until the last stroke has thrummed away into silence.

This old bird-friend of man has become almost as civilized as ourselves. But there are birds more wild and shy among us. The nighthawk (which is not really a hawk at all but a relative of the noisy whippoorwill) has found that an ideal place to lay its eggs is the flat top of a city apartment building. It doesn't make a nest; it just deposits on the roof its two eggs spotted over with pebbly marks. The roofs of city apartment houses are usually covered with a coat of tar paper and gravel, and the eggs blend in beautifully. Indeed, the bird has fewer enemies up there on the housetop than in the wild, and, swooping around the street lights pursuing the insects that collect there, he finds the city good to him.

In wilderness days, the chimney swifts used to nest in hollow trees when they could find them. Today they almost all nest in our chimneys. In early dawn, if you are up on the roof of some city building, you can sometimes see the swifts arising, sweetly chittering as they mount up into the pale skies. They spend their time on the wing, pursuing insects with a speed few but the duck hawk can surpass. When they wish to return to their nests in the chimney, they plunge accurately and suddenly into the sooty depths. And why, you wonder, are not the babies smoked out by the furnace fires? Because by the time the fires are lighted in autumn, the chimney swifts have raised their families and flown away on their long migration to the tropics.

So, all about the city-dweller, moves the deep current of life—not just the stream of traffic, the endless pedestrians passing. Sparrows and starlings and pigeons are plentiful, rats and mice run in their underworld, and the creatures of the sweet free wild make their astonishing entrances into the city fortress. A badger was recently discovered burrowing into a bank under the Michigan Boulevard Bridge, right by the Wrigley Building in downtown Chicago! No badger had been known in the neighborhood for almost a century. But this is a solitary and suspicious animal, that keeps out of sight as much as he can. So who knows how long a badger family may have been lurking there?

Generations of barn owls have lived in the turrets of the old Smithsonian Building in Washington. Weasels find their murderous way into chicken yards in any big town. Gray squirrels in every city park have learned to adapt themselves to our ways, and make the most successful little beggars in the world. Safe from hunters, squirrel populations in the city are probably denser than those in the country. Nature, then, is not a place apart. It is the world we live in. And, like the redskin long ago in his wilderness, we are a part of it forever.

THE ANIMAL PARADE

THIS fellowship with the animals is easy to feel when you trace your barking dog down the street or when you stroke a sleepy kitten till it purrs. A warm current of friendliness runs between you and the brother creature with a heart beating like your own under its soft hide. You can see, too, that you depend on animals like the Indians of the wilderness for many daily needs. When you eat your breakfast bacon or slip into a woolen sweater or put on your leather shoes, you have an animal to thank, every time.

But life, the miraculous gift, is bestowed far more generously than just on man and the beasts he lives with. It has been reckoned, you will remember, that there are about seven hundred thousand known species of animals now living on this spinning

30

globe which is our common home. Only a comparative few of them are the kind that a person usually means when he says "animal." He is apt to mean a warm-blooded, furry or hairy creature, the kind that brings forth its young alive (instead of laying eggs) and feeds them, at first, on mother's milk. That's a mammal, of course, one of the "higher" animals, as they are sometimes called.

But when a naturalist uses the word "animal," he means any living thing that is not a plant. He means:

The four-footed, warm-blooded mammals.

The two-legged, feathered birds.

The four-footed, cold-blooded turtles and lizards, salamanders and frogs.

The six-legged insects.

The eight-legged spiders.

The millipedes and centipedes which are supposed to have a hundred legs (well, a hundred more or *less!*)

The no-legged fishes and snakes.

The no-backbone creatures which include not only insects and spiders, but a lot of ocean life such as the octopus, jellyfish, starfish, crab, lobster, the sea anemones (which look confusingly like deep-sea flowers), the corals, the sponges, and so many more that I can't list them now.

They are all alive, just as much alive as you and I are although this common spark has been developed in them to various degrees and in endlessly different and curious ways. In each runs that power which is not light, nor fire, nor electricity, but is more marvelous and exciting than any of these. How long this life lasts varies among the animals as much as everything else. Of course

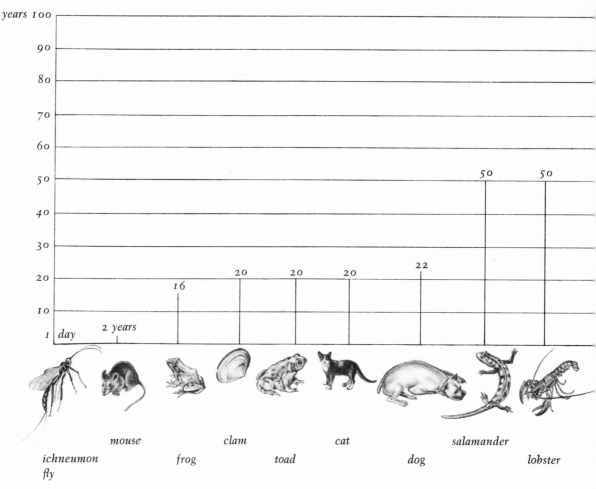

years 100

90

80

70

60

50   50   50

40

30

22

20   20   20   20

16

10

1 day   2 years

mouse   clam   cat   salamander

ichneumon   frog   toad   dog   lobster
fly

in the dangerous world of the wild, an existence can be cut short suddenly. But among the creatures that succeed in reaching a ripe old age, the span of it differs astonishingly.

How old, then, is "old"? A lively grandmother or a brisk gentleman of seventy will say, "You're just as old as you feel," which has some cheerful truth in it. But a cat near twenty doesn't feel much like mouse-hunting any more, and the field mouse itself finds life too much for it before it can finish its second winter. On the other hand, the lowly sea anemone, a creature very simply constructed, endures astonishingly; a well-known English biologist kept one in his laboratory for sixty-six years! A long life, but not a very merry

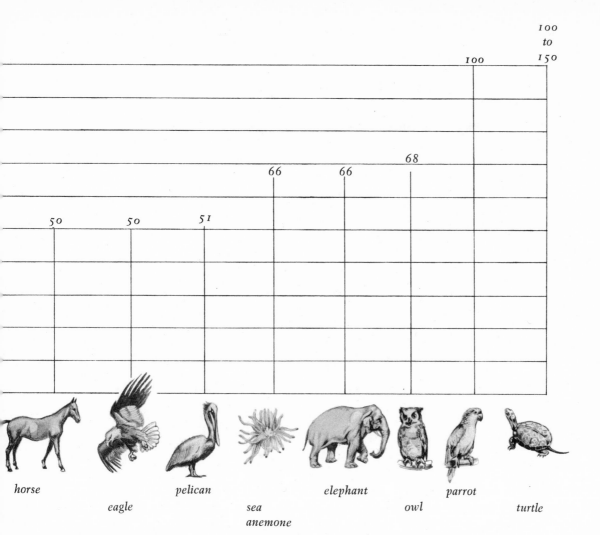

68

66   66

50   50   51

horse

eagle

pelican

sea
anemone

elephant

owl

parrot

turtle

one. For a sea anemone spends most of its time attached to a rock; when it does creep, on its one "foot" or pedal disk, it goes so slowly you cannot see it move.

A Mayfly, though it lives as a fly but a day or so, has a life of light and air and dancing activity. A clam can live fifteen to twenty years, but who wants to be a clam? A salamander may live half a century, but it doesn't see much of the world. An eagle can live as long as that, but soaring over mountain and forest it reaches heights of adventure and experience impossible to the cold-blooded salamanders. Thus length is no measure for life. It is what you get out of it, and what you put into it, that matters.

Yet to all creatures able to realize it, existence is so precious that they will struggle or fight to the end to preserve it. And the habitual winners at the great game of endurance provoke in us a wondering admiration. So it comes about that people are apt to exaggerate the ages of old animals. It is hard to be accurate, too, about creatures in the wild. The records kept of animals in captivity are more dependable. Even so, it is a temptation to boast about a pet's age; it may have been so long in the family that no one is very sure any more just how old it is. Parrots are often confidently said to live to be a hundred, but there is no real proof of that; they probably have lives half as long. The elephant too is commonly thought to grow as old as he is big, but no one has ever learned of an elephant known to have been older than sixty-nine.

But that *is* old, very old, for an animal. The record age for a horse is fifty years, for an owl sixty-eight, for a dog twenty-two, for a toad twenty, for a lobster fifty, for a pelican fifty-one, for a bullfrog sixteen. The creature that beats all the records for sheer endurance is the giant land tortoise. It is generally accepted that these slow old hard-shells can live a hundred years, perhaps a hundred and fifty. A long time to go crawling about the earth, your blood running chill and sluggish, with no braver way to meet danger than to draw into your shell!

It is better, a man will feel, to stand upright on two feet and face the world for as long as it may be granted him to enjoy it. And this is longer than any other mammal is allowed. Even the wrinkled elephant is second to man in longevity. With every year's discoveries in medicine and science, too, the human span is prolonged. Well may we give thanks, walking the crowded world, for our own generous share of the grand adventure!

THE GREEN KINGDOM

BESIDE the most ancient of living things, even man, even the venerable tortoise, are mere youngsters. Their lives, comparatively, are as brief as the Mayfly's. For plants, too, are alive—as alive as animals in their own ways—and there is no age like the grand, calm age of a tree.

In the mountains of California, in the mighty range called the Sierra Nevada, stand the bigtrees, or giant sequoias, the oldest living things in all the world. Some of them are over three thousand years old and look it, with their grave, evergreen foliage, their reddish bark, their tremendous trunks sometimes as much as thirty feet in diameter.

35

There are two kinds of sequoias, or redwoods, and the other kind also grows in California but on the northern coast where the fog drifts in from the Pacific Ocean and the long sunbeams slant angelically through it. Here rise the groves of the sequoia called everlasting, and these coast redwoods are even taller than the mountain kind, two hundred, three hundred, feet tall—and more.

Every year that a tree grows, it makes another ring of cells under the bark of its trunk. When a tree is cut down, its age can be reckoned by counting the rings that show at the butt end of the log. One sequoia log was felled in 1932, and its annual growth rings have been marked to show its age at various points of history's march past it. The tree probably first pushed up from the forest floor in the year 700. It was already 366 years old when William the Conqueror invaded England. Its somber, sweeping branches were lofty when Columbus came sailing toward our shores. By the time it fell under slashing steel, it had lived over ten centuries.

When a redwood is cut down, the stump often sprouts again

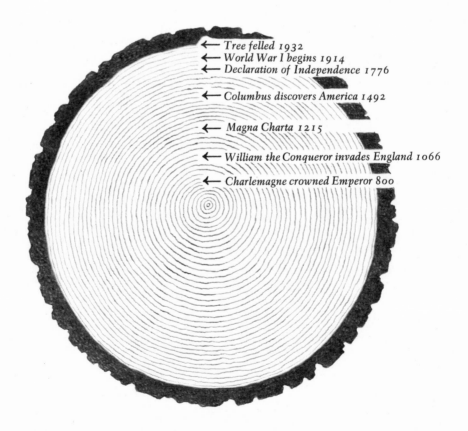

←— Tree felled 1932
←— World War I begins 1914
←— Declaration of Independence 1776

←— Columbus discovers America 1492

←— Magna Charta 1215

←— William the Conqueror invades England 1066

←— Charlemagne crowned Emperor 800

from the base in a circle of graceful daughter trees. Even a fallen log may send up shoots. No wonder such a tree is called everlasting. It is practically immortal. And walking along the misty aisles of a redwood forest, down ferny paths between giant boles, you feel close to some great secret. The wind in the branches far overhead seems to say *Hush*, and again *Hush!* It is like a vast, calm breathing. Here life goes quietly on forever.

It is the same life that runs through all the vegetable kingdom, which has, you'll remember, about three hundred thousand kinds of citizens. These range in size all the way from a bigtree to a yeast plant, which is just one, single cell, forever budding and branching. You wouldn't think that a cake of yeast belonged with the vegetables, would you? But it is composed of millions of one-celled yeast plants which, giving off bubbles of carbon dioxide gas, raise the baker's bread loaf. Simple, too, are the algae, which

you know as the green or brown scum that floats on stagnant ponds and ditches. These are humble cousins of the seaweeds that range from the vivid, lace-like bits you can pick up on the beach to others the size of tall trees, towering and wavering under the ocean waters.

And lowly but powerful plants are the molds. You have probably seen mold growing on stale bread and noticed that it looks like a tiny blue-green or black forest. Penicillium is the name of a common mold that yields us the wonder-drug penicillin, saver of many lives. Molds belong in the class of the fungi, those stealthy and elfin plants that you find especially in the woods after an autumn rain. They appear then, as though by earthly magic, as red-capped toadstools marching along a log, or as spongy brackets growing from a tree trunk, or those puffballs among the fallen leaves that send out a cloud of "smoke" when you tap them.

Fantastical, too, are the lichens sprawling out on the rocks like gray-green maps of imaginary continents. Or some hang from the trees like gray beards waving in the wind. They are even more curious than they look, for they are really composed of *two* plants living together in partnership—an alga and a fungus.

But no part of the green world seems so much out of fairyland as the sub-kingdom of the mosses. Some are soft as deep velvet under your stroking hand; some look like very tiny woodlands when you bend close to them. Others, when they are lifted dripping from a pool, are so delicate the light shines through them. One gray, lacy bog moss—eaten by reindeer in the north—is used a great deal for wrapping around plants from a nursery to keep the roots moist; its name is sphagnum. To me the names of many of the mosses sound like a band of gnomes in a fairy tale—Sphagnum, Hypnum, Bryum, Mnium, and Grimmia.

Have you noticed that these lowlier citizens of the plant kingdom are most of them flattish and almost all flabby? They are like the no-backbone members of the animal kingdom. And most of them, like the jellyfish and the sea anemones, live in or near water or at least in damp surroundings. But now, with the next class, the ferns, we come to the first plants that can really stand up straight, for they have woody strands of strengthening tissue in their stems. They are the first that can spread out broad leaves, since veins of fiber run through the foliage too. They seem modest, graceful plants now, seldom (outside the tropics) more than knee-high, and shyly they grow in moist, dim, shady places. Nor are there a great many species of ferns left in the world today. But once upon a time—a little matter of three hundred million years ago!—ferns dominated the scenery of this planet. They grew in vast abundance, some tall as trees. In the strange, warm damp of that long-ago world they flourished, and cast their fertility upon the wind,

and fell. What we dig up today as coal are the fossilized remains of those fern forests.

Ferns have no flowers, and in the far, dim times when they were masters of the earth there was never a blossom to delight the eye or to lure a bee by perfume or color. (There wasn't a bee yet, either!) When flowering plants appeared, they rather swiftly mastered the whole globe and crowded the ferns out of their kingship. Today every corner of earth, except the ocean where seaweeds still rule and the biggest lakes, is dominated by the kind of plant that bears flowers. True that some of these flowers are so tiny they are scarcely noticeable, but this highest form of plant life has become everywhere triumphant. The pollen from it rises high, even above the city skyscraper; in the days of primeval America clouds of pollen swept from the great forests a hundred miles or more out to sea. The seeds of flowering plants, if little and light and provided with down as dandelion and cattail seeds are, can go sailing away on a strong wind for great distances. Birds carry seeds on their migrations across seas, and so the flowering clans have traveled and settled over all the earth.

Humans have played their part in this for centuries. An ancient Egyptian picture shows a queen directing the transplanting of some trees from a foreign land into the ships which are to carry them back to her country. In our own historical times, the colonists from the Old World brought with them to this new land, plants from their home gardens—stocks and pinks, apples and pears. When the pioneers crossed the plains westward, in the covered wagons along with the chests and bedsteads went slips of loved old rosebushes. And today the commerce in flowering plants is world-wide. So many lovely aliens have rooted contentedly among us and become our own. In any American garden in autumn you will find

the zinnia, the sacred flower of the Aztec Indians, who cultivated
it centuries ago in Mexico. Here is a geranium from South Africa,
and there are nasturtiums from South America, both so common
with us now that we take them for granted.

Yet for all their journeying, flowers have a way of speaking to
us intimately of the place that they, and we, call home. The man

lonely for Scotland remembers the "bonny purple heather"; the Japanese loves his cherry blossoms. The serene lotus blossom is India's flower; the rose has been England's ever since the War of the Roses. The sweet breath of a flower can say more than human lips, and so the orange blossom is symbol to us of a wedding. It is

also the state flower of Florida. California has adopted its golden poppy, Texas has its gay bluebonnets, Kansas its sunflower, Colorado its airy blue columbine. So flowers have come not only to triumph in Nature, but to captivate the human heart with their form and scent and radiance of color.

II.

EACH

A

REALM

THE DESERT

Oᴜʀ country, the United States of America, lies spread out upon the map like a flag unfurled in a strong wind. There in a grand rough checkerboard lie the forty-eight states, and anyone can find his own and feel pride in being a citizen of Illinois or California, Vermont or Montana. But these lines were drawn by history; they are not natural borders. In natural history—the study of life out-of-doors—we see America composed rather of mountain ranges and great plains, of deserts and Christmas-tree forests, of lake country and swamp country and farming country.

The people of Kansas and the folk of Maine are not so very different after all. They can travel about and make a comfortable home anywhere in the land. Not so the creatures of the natural

49

provinces. Each region has its own way of life. Anywhere that you live, if you look around you, lies a complex little natural society. What it is like, of course, depends on the environment.

Sometimes you have to look hard to discover it. Perhaps you have traveled, by train or car, across the vast, arid lands that lie between the Rocky Mountains and the coast of California with its palms and orange groves. It is always exciting to go out West for the first time; you feel like a pioneer, watching the country open out, wide and rugged and free, in glowing colors of old red and gold like Indian war paint. The sky seems higher here, and the towns are far apart, lying plain and low under that deep blue dome. There are fewer and fewer of them as you cross New Mexico and Arizona. Sometimes you see a cowboy riding lonely after his cattle, and you see Indians too, Navahos, watching their sheep or squatting by their odd round houses called hogans. But the world

seems to get emptier and emptier. There is more sky than land. And now between the distant ranges the land is flat and barren of all but dull, scrubby growth, stretching out and out to a limitless horizon. You are in the desert.

Here, you may say to yourself, there is surely nothing alive, nothing but those gray-green, uninteresting bushes. This is the dullest waste place I ever saw! How soon do we get out of it?

Well, if you ever get really *into* it, you will find it full of strange and beautiful life. The fascination of the desert becomes a spell. From the time that he wakes in the vast glow of dawn to the hoarse cawing of ravens, till he falls asleep hearing the distant "singing" of coyotes in the deep night, discovery absorbs a naturalist.

For this "empty" country is jumping with liveliness. Champion in that line is the jack rabbit. He jumps like a jack out of the box. He can jump, at one bound, over twenty feet, and go on for miles

in hops like that. Every leap takes him a couple of feet into the air, though he can go higher, clearing a fence as much as five feet high. His long mulish ears can catch the least sound of an enemy—coyote, desert fox, weasel, rattlesnake, or eagle, and off he goes! Or he may escape by hiding in plain sight. He has a trick of "freezing," stopping absolutely still, as you do in the game of Red Light. Then the soft gray-brown of his fur merges with the desert earth and with the stems of the common desert plants, the creosote bush and the cactus.

The pack rat is as busy as the jack. You see him less easily, but you know he's been around when you find something missing from your camp—a comb, or a trinket, or maybe a pocket mirror. Where on earth can it have gone? Who would have taken it? You find the answer if you discover the pack rat's nest. It is often full of such trifles which have caught the fancy of this big-eared, gentle little creature. He is often called the trade rat, because he has a way of leaving something in the place from which he has filched some-

thing else. This is not really because he means to make an exchange, but because he has an aimless, ridiculous way of picking up sticks or bits of rubbish, carrying them awhile and then dropping them somewhere else.

The mammals of the desert are most active at night, and it is easiest to see them then, when you can catch the gleam of their eyes in the dark, reflecting your electric torch or car lights. By day it is the birds you can watch. That long-necked, chicken-sized fowl pacing your automobile along the road, a lizard he hasn't had time

to swallow still dangling from his bill, is a roadrunner. That long-tailed bird with a slightly downbent beak, which swoops right into the most prickly cactus of all, is a cactus wren; she has built her nest down there, protected by the fierce spines from thieving owl or shrike. Hummingbirds dart by in the blazing air, their throat feathers flashing colored fire. A slow old desert tortoise crawls through the hot sand. A raven's shadow floats over it. A rattlesnake lies coiled in the shade of a rock, waiting for twilight before gliding forth upon its business. All across the desert this secret activity goes on, in this hot, bright, pantingly thirsty place where there is no cool pool, no running stream for refreshment.

But the birds know where they can catch a few sips and fly far to drink at such spots. For some tiny creatures, the dew that falls at night is water enough. The desert tortoise carries water around with him in two sacs under his shell. And some animals, like the jack rabbit, never take a drink all their lives long! They get the water they need out of what they eat. Naturally, then, one of the favorite foods of the jack is the giant cactus, or saguaro, for this tree-sized vegetable is 90 per cent water, and as the main trunk may weigh five or six tons, a big old saguaro is nothing less than

a magnificent reservoir in a column as much as forty feet high. The rind of such a cactus is pleated, so to speak, and this makes it elastic. When the desert rains fall, the great soft elastic stem is thus able to plump out full of water, the "pleats" practically disappearing.

Protected by a fearful armament of spines, the saguaro is safe from most desert animals, but the jack rabbit is a tough and determined character. He worms his soft nose dauntlessly between the clusters of spines, near the base of the giant cactus, until he can slide his chisel teeth under the rind. Once he has gained the first tooth-hold, the rest is easy; he can undermine, strip, and guzzle as he pleases. Where one rabbit has burgled his way in, another thirsty jack will soon follow. Little it matters to them if at last they topple this plant king of the desert.

Able to go without water for a long time because they are thus able to store it, the cacti are the vegetable camels of our land. Though they are native to the deserts of our Western Hemisphere —and only there—sometimes they look like inhabitants of some other and harsher planet. What leaves they have are so small as to be scarcely noticeable. They may be tall as trees, but they have no trunk of solid wood. Their stems and branches are often flattened and so weirdly jointed that the plants look as though they were threatening you or gesturing in despair.

And their spines are truly to be dreaded. Some are fine as bristles, but a hundred of these may stick you at once. Others are long and stiff and sharp as a porcupine's quills. Yet others are backwardly barbed like fishhooks so that they hurt even more coming out than going in! Worst, perhaps, is the jumping cholla. The joints of its spiny balls are so loosely connected with the plant that the merest touch, or even the hoofbeats of a passing horse, causes them practically to jump off the bush. But the pack rat seems not to fear it; his nest is often surrounded by a ring of these prickly balls. Whether he collects them for protection or whether they happen to fall there, they form a mine field that few creatures care to cross.

Yet when the cacti blossom, all must be forgiven them. It is as though a thousand brilliant water lilies, white and yellow, rose and red, had come to perch on the cruel leafless cactus branches in the midst of the waterless desert. Many of these blazing blossoms open in the night when the desert is at its coolest. One such, the night-blooming cereus, blooms on only one or two nights in the whole year. As the petals open in little jerks and slips, an exquisite odor steals forth that may scent the air for a hundred feet around, luring the moths to come. Then by the time the sun lifts its blazing rim over the level horizon, the flower of the cereus is already closing. No wonder that the Spanish-speaking people in that desert country call this *Reina de la Noche*—Queen of the Night.

THE POND

SPRING comes early to the seasonal pond as it brims with the last of winter's melted snows, reflecting a mild sky. Fed by no running stream but only by snow and rain and drainage from the surrounding fields or woods, the pond is filled nevertheless with fiercely active life. It is a special kind of life that must be able both to flourish in the chill, still waters of spring and to endure through August drought, when the pond is only a cracked floor of dry mud. So it has developed many a trick of vanishing in plain sight, or turning itself into something else, or just going to sleep through hard times.

Now, in early April, the pond is coming awake. The year's first flush of color is on the limber twigs of the bordering willows where soon the silvery "pussies" will appear. The warming water is green

58

with pond scum or algae, those very simple plants that are floating pasturage for countless tiny nibbling pond-dwellers. The first
music of the year, too, comes from the pond—the thin, high
creak-croak of the many spring peepers and swamp tree-frogs. It
is a sound both lonely and sociable, contented and full of name-
less sadness, a song that swells the singer's throat till it is nearly
the size of his little frog body. Soon now the bright air will ring
with the metallic whistle of the red-winged blackbirds up from
the south where they are called soldier birds because of their
shoulder patches that flash red and yellow.

April was the time, when I was a boy, that I used to go squelch-ing out to the pond armed with a cloth net on a long pole and a number of empty jam jars. Every spring I made a fresh-water aquarium lively with creatures scooped up on these expeditions and set with pond plants to provide them with oxygen. My pond-dwellers were worth watching, for such waters are a place of magical transformations. Many of the animals go through stages, each completely different from the last. That floating blob of cloudy jelly, for instance, is a mass of frog's eggs. The velvety dark spots in it will presently turn into a crowd of tiny tadpoles, wrigglers mostly mouth. In a few short weeks they will grow legs, lose their tails, and turn into frogs that, when the pond waters shrink and stagnate, can jump away as lively landlubbers.

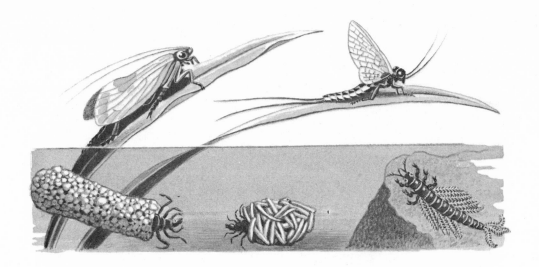

Most of the pond insects, too, lead double lives, under water and in the air. Down on the oozy bottom the caddis worm crawls along dragging after it the queer little house it builds out of bits of stick and stone held together with silk. Then one day it seals itself in to undergo a mysterious change. After a fortnight it breaks out, swims to the surface, walks on the top of the water till it finds some plant to climb up on, and there it is transformed into a delicate yellow-and-black caddisfly that takes wing into summery air. The Mayfly leads a double life much like that, shedding its outer skin when it comes to the surface before it flies off for its few hours of winged existence, during which it will not even eat, for it has no mouth parts. And the immature little savage that lurks on the muddy bottom ready to seize any prey swimming past is a very different form from the brilliant adult dragonfly flashing like a fairy jet plane over the surface, yet they are one and the same creature, in two stages of life.

That surface of the pond is not only a ceiling to some aquatic animals but a floor to others. The tension of it creates an invisible film, slightly tougher than the rest of the water, and on this the

water-striders go walking, just dimpling the surface at each step. These are bugs that have waxy hairs on their feet enabling them to go skating over the water film without either breaking through or getting wet. The dytiscus beetle, on the other hand, goes easily down into the pond, enclosed in a silvery bubble of air like a diver taking compressed air in an aqualung. Both these insects survive the pond's seasonal changes by hibernating at the bottom of it, which is why you will find them among the first to be up and about in spring. Then, too, the pond is thronged with delicate fairy shrimp that swim gracefully along on their backs with a rippling of their double rows of legs. These rainbow-colored tiny crustaceans lay their eggs and die before the pond dries up. But the eggs survive, and may even blow away like dust, to start a new lot of fairy shrimps to paddling happily through other waters.

By the time the fairy shrimps have vanished, the cattails are tall in the marshy bays of the pond. It is there, or in the bulrushes, that the redwings like to nest. These talkative and excitable black-birds sometimes make a whole series of false or incomplete nests,

as well as the finished ones, which gives to the cattail marsh the look of a redwing village. The eggs have long been hatched and the pond is drowsing in summer shimmer when the cattail seeds begin to break from the brown velvet spikes and float away on their downy parachutes. The Ojibwa Indians called that fluff by a name meaning "it flies around." The Potawatomies called it "fruit for baby's bed," and they stuffed quilts and pillows with it, as well as plaiting the cattail leaves for mats.

Amid the rushes and cattails there is often a bird that you look at without seeing it. This is the bittern, called by some country people "stake driver," because one of his notes sounds like a stake being driven into squelchy mud. A hump-shouldered big brown bird, he has when alarmed a trick of standing so still, with his long bill pointed upward, that he is all but invisible in plain sight. You notice him only when he suddenly lifts and flaps away, uttering a hoarse cry. The heron comes to the pond, too, trailing long legs, alighting with a balance of great wings. Quick as a snake its neck uncoils to snap up a leaping frog or any crayfish unwary enough to have crawled out of its curious mud chimney.

Hot and bright the August sun blazes over the diminishing water. The algae lie in scummy streaks along the hard-dried shores. Now sometimes you will find one of the pond's chief inhabitants wandering off as if in disgust. This is the snapping turtle, a lazy but pugnacious fellow that grows to as much as a foot long. He has idled the past months away basking for hours on a log adrift in the pond, or lying afloat at the warm surface, or burrowing in the rich mud at the bottom where he spent the winter asleep. On land he is an even slower poke; I used to catch him easily and lightly carve the date and my initials on his hard, unfeeling shell. Years later I'd meet him again and know him

for an old friend. But be careful if you pick up one of these creatures to carry him by the tail and hold him well away from your body. He earned his name of snapping turtle by a bite that hurts.

The autumn rains persuade the turtles that the pond is home after all. Snipe and plovers and sandpipers may come then to peck and poke at the rising edge of the water, and teetering yellowlegs keep their flock together with little clinking cries. Soon now the leopard frogs go hopping back to the place where they were tadpoles, croaking their pilgrims' chorus as they hobble through the grass. Common throughout our country, this spotty frog is the likeliest one to catch, easy to keep and even to tame, for it needs little water. Thus it is able to migrate every summer to the fields, returning regularly in autumn to the pond, where it hibernates. And here in spring it breeds, and once again are set afloat those cloudy masses of frog's eggs.

So the seasonal pond lives, by the cycle of wet and dry. It is a half-world, half in the water, half out. Most of its dwellers know how to make the best of both worlds and enjoy each one in its season—a lesson for anyone who likes to turn everything into a lesson!

THE MEADOW

MIDSUMMER is the year at high tide. Life is easy and lazy and full. The beginning of school is still too far away to think about, and the days are still long enough for you to do whatever you want to do. Yet they are so warm and bright that you don't want to do much of anything. It's enough just to lie in the shade of the big oak in the summer meadow, and look at a sky clear of all but wandering white puffs of cloud, and listen to the great breathing silence around you.

But the sky isn't really empty, you notice. There is a hawk hovering there as though hung aloft on invisible threads. And the silence is full of tiny sounds, chirps and humming and soft stirrings. Real emptiness and silence would be deathy; you could have them on the moon, and you would hate them. Instead, all

around you is the living world, enjoying the same rich and peaceful moment of the year that makes you so contented. Now the feverish activity of spring, with its mating and nesting and rearing of young, is over. Now there is plenty for all, and autumn with its chill and changes is yet to come.

A bobolink lights on a tall stalk of goldenrod coming into flower, but he has nothing to say for himself. For in summer most of the birds fall silent, one by one, and many begin to moult. Once in a while the meadowlark tosses his windy whistle from a fence post, and when some goldfinch crosses the meadow on his billowing flight he may trill as he flies, like the wild canary he is. And perhaps you can hear, from high in the trees overhead, a thin, high, hungry screaming. That will be the fledglings of some second nesting, for a few birds raise two families a year.

But most of the music of late summer is furnished by the tiny orchestra in the grass—the grasshoppers, katydids, and crickets. The meadow is lively with 'hoppers that shoot high over the grasses propelled by their strong hind legs. True that a grasshopper has a double set of wings, the outer leathery, the inner gauzy, but he can scarcely flutter these and uses them rather for gliding. He also fiddles with them. The toothed edge of one hind leg is rubbed against the ridges on a wing in a serenade to his lady. She listens, all ears, but these ears are not like ours, not even in her head, but are situated just below her knees!

The cricket performs in much the same fashion. He lifts his wings and, with his right one over his left, produces chirps so loud and high-pitched as to startle you if you are near. And, by pressing his wings against his side, he can make these chirps seem to come from a dozen different directions as a ventriloquist can "throw" his voice. In China and Japan the cricket is admired as

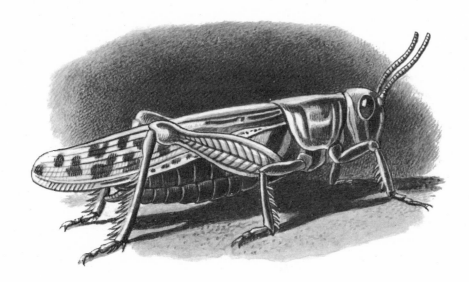

a musician and kept as a pet in tiny cages. There he not only sings for his supper but is led forth to fight other crickets in exhibition matches, and heavy bets are laid on favorite cricket champions. Uncaged, in a free American meadow, a cricket may hop a hundred times the length of his body. That's liberty for you!

To hear the katydid contradict himself, you must wait till twilight. With two rasps of the sharp edge of one wing on the file of another, he says that "Katy did" and with three rasps insists "Katy didn't." This may go on all night, for some scientist who likes to do arithmetic has figured that during a summer season one katydid may scrape its wings together between thirty and fifty million times. And still the argument isn't settled!

Now at midday in the meadow you'll hear instead a high, rising, sizzling note that dies away in an eerie wail. That's a cicada, which is not a fiddler but a drummer. From somewhere up in the oak tree he sends out that long whirring note, produced by muscularly vibrating little drums in his side, much as you can make a noise by pushing in and out the flexible bottom of a pan. You are less

likely to see the drumming cicada than to find his cast-off skin
still clinging, with a ghostly look of life, to the bark of the tree
where he split it down the back and emerged from it with wings
ready to take the air. That discarded form he wore during the long
time that he lived underground as a grub or larva—two years, if
he is the common "dog-day" cicada.

The rustling in the grass, which even on a windless day you
may hear if you have been a long time quiet, may be a striped
garter snake, most harmless of little reptiles. Or it may be one of
the many mouse people on his scurrying business. For any meadow
is crisscrossed with mouse runways; with his sharp teeth the
meadow mouse gnaws down the grasses to make a path an inch
or so wide, and under the tall sheltering grasses that arch overhead he scampers unseen. He makes burrows in the field, too,
where he may have his nest, or he fashions the nest, a round little
affair of woven grasses, in some snug nook above ground. Here,
there are almost always mice children to be found, squirming as
naked as pink worms when they are first born, for the meadow
mice breed all the year round.

The result is, of course, mice and mice and more mice. Yet there seem never too many to satisfy the hungers of the creatures that like mouse for dinner—cats, skunks, dogs, weasels, coyotes, crows, opossums, snakes, owls, and many others. And though mouse is the principle item of diet for so many creatures, there yet occur great mouse years—seasons of unexplained overpopulation when the meadow is crowded with nests, and the little scurriers can be seen running even in the open roads.

Shyer than this blunt-nosed cousin is the white-footed or deer mouse, an appealing little animal with large dark eyes and the quaint habit of making its summer home in some discarded bird's nest. Sometimes this is roofed over with cattail down, and a hole is nibbled at the bottom for a door. Sheltered here when the south

wind gently sways the bush where the nest clings, the deer mouse passes the season of warmth and abundance, finding plentiful seeds and berries at hand. Nor does he fear winter, when he makes another home safe underground or in some grass-lined hollow in a tree and snuggles up in cosy rows with his brothers to sleep out the cold.

But no one, on a fine August day, worries about that time, least of all the shrew, who lives excitably one meal and one moment at a time. This is the tiniest mammal in the world, and the hungriest. Looking like a mouse but with a pointed head and nose, he is almost never still, for nerves and hunger drive him. He has to be eating all the time, or he would drop dead. He manages to consume his own weight in food every three hours! Imagine eating as much as you weigh for breakfast, and the same amount again for luncheon, and as much more at early dinner time!

The shrew is principally an insect eater, and thus useful to man. And that hawk lazily floating over the meadow is the kind that likes mice and rats, and so he too is a good friend to the farmer who owns this field. You can tell in a glance that he is not one of the chicken-eating hawks, for that kind have longer and narrower tails. The broad-tailed hawks are all welcome, and help to keep down the population of mice that get into the barn and devour the grain or eat it even in the field.

"Good" or "bad," "useful" or "harmful"—they are man-made words and fit only a human way of thinking. Going about his barnyard, the farmer naturally finds them in his mind when he glances at the distant hawk in the sky or scans the sunny field and figures on what the hay will bring him. But under the tree in the meadow there seems to be room for hawk and mouse, shrew and grasshopper, and the wide blue sky smiles down on all of them equally.

THE BARN

You are lucky if ever you knew and loved, as I have, a big old barn, with wide doors open at each end and a summer wind scented with clover stirring the fringe of hay. Such a barn is as fascinating a treasure box for the naturalist as a sea chest filled with strange cargo from afar. For the barn also holds treasure brought from ancient times and faraway kingdoms, inhabited as it is by some of the best-loved creatures in the world.

And the farmyard outside, around the barn, has foreign wonders in it too. There the common rooster greets the day with the same cry his wild ancestors raised in the jungles of India. He is as truly exotic (a word that just means "foreign") as the gaudy plumage and gibberish of some old sailor's parrot. So are the gabbling guinea hens, who originated in Africa. Yet nothing is more lovably American than such an old-fashioned barn and yard.

I say "old-fashioned" because on many of the up-to-date farms agriculture and stock-raising have become so scientific that it is harder to discover any natural history on them. The cows, kept in sterilized stalls, are milked by machinery. The horse and mule may have given way to the tractor. Even the hens lay their eggs without benefit of rooster. Modern scientific farming is much to be admired, but I am glad that there remains to us, here and there in country corners, many an old-style barn, with haylofts where children can romp or tell secrets while the dust motes dance in the long sharp sunbeams.

There you may come to know the barn swallow, living spirit of the barn itself. Steel-blue above, with a breast of cinnamon, it comes skimming through the wide-open doors and sweeps up with

a contented twitter to its nest fixed in a crotch of the broad, dusty beams. The swallow is the happiest of links between the wild and the domestic. In the days when our land was wilderness, these swallows nested, like the chimney swifts, in hollow trees or in caves. The coming of the settler offered them a new and better home site, and they repay the shelter of the farmer's barn by devouring quantities of his worst insect enemies: chinch bugs, boll weevils, stink bugs, leaf bugs, cutworms, May beetles, leaf-rollers, and the coddling moths and cankerworm moths that spoil the apples and apple trees.

These gentle, swift-winged hunters make war too on the wood-boring beetles and the carpenter ants whose secret galleries eat the heart out of the barn timbers. Over and over they swiftly patrol the farm pond, ridding it of mosquitoes. But practically never do barn swallows eat our insect benefactors, the honeybees and the ladybugs, carab beetles and dragonflies which prey on those other insects the farmer calls pests. Instead they dart among the cattle, consuming the hateful flies that torment the beasts, or flash after the reaper in the field to catch whatever insects its blades beat up. Seldom do you see a swallow still; even in drinking it does not stop but sweeps up a sip as it skims the water.

One swallow doesn't make a summer, but a courting pair spells springtime. For hours and days the female leads her swain a sort of game of kiss-tag, which ends when she is sure she is sought by the fastest swallow in the world. Then she waits in the hay-sweet dusk of the eaves for him to come close and nestle his head against hers. Soon, like any engaged couple looking for a house, the two set off—always at top speed—to flash in and out the barn, cutting and curving through the sunshine like airy knives till they have found a spot safe enough from the rats and prowling barn cat.

Then you may see the mated pair dash to the edge of the farm pond to scoop up pellets of mud with their bills. But you can't make bricks without straw, says the Bible, and so they add straw from the barn floor, and mixing this with the mud, they fashion a nest, in shape like a big coffee cup, up on the chosen beam in the velvet shadows. This home, soon filled with eggs and then babies, they will defend dauntlessly. Armed only with love and courage, they send the cat flying with her ears pinned back and will even chase a hawk not only out of the barnyard but over the horizon.

Like the barn swallows, the mud-dauber wasps gather clay from the pond margin to make their nest under the beams. The individual cells of the nest are tubular and the whole cluster of cells hangs from a sort of stalk, like some flower-head upside down. And the mud-dauber herself is a long-stalked creature, the waist almost as thin as a needle, the abdomen like a steel-blue bobbin. You may venture very close to the nest, if you move slowly and don't jar the beam, to watch the dauber building her strange mud-castle. Again like the swallow, the dauber wasp is a tireless enemy of the farmer's insect foes, for she slays them in their grub or caterpillar stages when they do their worst work.

Many an old barn has its owl family too. The true barn owl, a big kindly, white and yellowish creature with no fierce look in his eyes, is lacking in the North Atlantic and Middle Western states, but he is known in the South Atlantic and above all in the Western states, as well as all over Europe. No cat was ever a better mouser or ratter. A barn owl near my house drops a pile of rodent bones every night under his favorite perch. These harmful rats and mice are his favorite diet, so if you have a barn owl in your barn you have a good neighbor. And an almost silent one; no eerie screech, no hoarse *woo-hoo* about him! His call is just a scratchy hiss now and then.

And all the time down in their stalls the cattle are placidly chewing their cuds, animals very unlike those from which they are descended by long lines of breeding that has been going on for thousands of years. These ancestors of theirs roamed wild upon the plains and through the woods of Europe in the days before history began. They were hunted and lassoed by the cave men, who drew pictures of them, existing today on cave walls in France and Spain. Those charging bulls and crowding cows look marvelously fierce and alive though they were painted some ten thousand years ago and more.

Egyptian wall paintings, made much later, show cattle being herded and driven along by peasants with whips. So we know that domestication of these beasts must have begun at least four or five thousand years ago. Two main sources still can be traced in our cattle. One is the aurochs, which was a great black or gray brute with a white stripe down his back, and long horns and a long face. The other is the short-horned Celtic breed of cattle, with shorter, broader face, shorter legs, reddish or tan coat, and no white stripe. Probably you can recognize traits of these two wild forms in the tame breeds you see today. At any rate, from these

two and crosses between them, we have bred for heavy milk production such dairy cattle as the black Holsteins and the ruddy brown Jerseys, and for beef such range cattle as the white-faced Herefords and the black Angus.

You might not think there was anything much to be learned about how and why a cow chews its cud, but it's the most important cog in the whole machinery of milk and beef production. For there is nothing as hard to digest as the tough cellulose fibers of grass. When Nebuchadnezzar, in the Old Testament, got down

on all fours and chewed the grass, he was considered insane—and rightly so. The human digestive tract just isn't made for such roughage. But cattle, buffalo, deer, elk, camels, yaks, sheep and goats, antelopes, and almost all the grazing animals go through a complex process to turn grass into mutton, wool, hides, bone, milk, steaks, and so on. To accomplish such digestion, most grazing animals, wild or domestic, need broad heavy teeth and two or even more stomachs, not to mention a sort of pre-stomach called the rumen where the cud is first softened with water.

What is the breed of the farm dog? If he knew his own family tree, he could boast that dogs have been in domestication longer than any other creature. The modern dog is probably a mixture of several wild canines, such as the wolf and jackal. From this mixture a great number of distinct breeds have appeared. The setters, spaniels, pointers, and retrievers are the favorites if the farmer is a quail- or duck-hunter. If he hunts mammals, he selects one of the scent hounds—the fox hound, basset, beagle, or harrier. If there are sheep or cattle to guard and herd, then he chooses one of the "working" dogs—collies and sheepdogs and German shepherds. When well trained, these canines perform wonders at herding, doing what it would take a dozen shepherd boys to accomplish.

And what a story there is in horses! The noblest type of farm horse is the powerful Belgian Percheron, fit to pull heavy wagons

but grown rare now in the days of machinery. Then there's the genuine cowboy's saddle horse, the quarter horse, used for working cattle on the western ranges and wonderfully obedient and steady-nerved. Where I live, in California, are bred the Golden Palominos, popular in circuses for their beauty. Kentucky prides itself on its racers descended from Arab steeds, every champion as carefully pedigreed as a king. These are just a few of the aristocrats of the horse family which began its evolution fifty million years ago in Wyoming as a creature not much bigger than a fox!

So one could continue on through the list of man's closest animal friends with the story of our geese, ducks, turkeys, guinea fowl, the races of pigeons (the fantails, the pouters, the tumblers). Man, when he lays his hand upon Nature, may destroy it ruthlessly, with fire and ax and flood, in greed or to build his cities. But through the ages, too, he has been a partner to her and has so improved many plants and animals that not only would he not part with them now, but they could not do without him.

THE FOREST

ONE hot, tired summer my three boys and I got out a map of our country. Away up in the left-hand corner of it lay the state of Washington, colored green as it ought to be, for it is one of the greenest and rainiest of all the forty-eight —indeed, it is called the Evergreen State. In the extreme north-west corner of it is the Olympic Peninsula, reaching up into cold northern waters and holding a mountain range, the Olympics, that lift everlasting snows high above wilderness. In the heart of the peninsula we located the Olympic National Park. That is the greatest tract of absolutely virgin forest left to us in the United States. And there lives the Roosevelt elk, king of all the deer family, as proud an animal as walks American soil.

So we set out, my wife and I and the boys, who were then ten, twelve, and fourteen years old. When you rush through the glittering metallic river of cars on our highways, past miles of billboards and hamburger stands and gas stations, you wonder if ever you will really reach a place of cool green calm. But after a thousand miles we found ourselves in the silent depths of an ageless forest. The air was sharp with unseen mountain snows and the breath of the Pacific, not far away. The trees were all coniferous— that is, the Christmas kind—and they grew so close together that their crowns locked overhead, their roots underfoot, with never a clearing, never a farm or even a house, not a human being to be seen dwelling among them. It is the rainfall—as much as one hundred to two hundred inches of it a year—that makes them grow so thick and tall, and brings the moss to gleam an eerie emerald upon their shadowy trunks.

These trees are some of the mightiest on earth. Grandest giants are the Douglas firs, which in stature are second only to the sequoias of California and rank first in all the world as a lumber tree. Here too were Sitka spruces, lofty and splendid as cathedral spires, with wood so strong in proportion to its very light weight that it is invaluable for making airplane propellers. Everywhere we heard the sighing of hemlocks and smelled the balsam incense of the tidelands fir. Somber canoe cedars let down their flat sprays of foliage; the scent of their fragrant wood is familiar to you if you have ever sniffed around a package of shingles when a new house is being roofed. The Indians of Alaska carved the great trunks of this tree into their totem poles; hollowing out the boles with fire, they made of this cedar their war canoes that could hold each one as many as forty men.

We all felt commanded to silence by the lordly trees that crowded close to the road and stretched away from it on either side mile upon mile into unknown depths of forest, with other trees, fallen years ago, lying log upon tangled log at the feet of the ranks still standing. These rooted giants ruled this place, and silence and stillness were law. The three boys grew as quiet as though a spell had fallen upon them, though sometimes an awed "Whew!" came through their lips, a sound like the murmur of the trees themselves.

And then, out of the woods and down the road, came the Roose-

velt elk—a whole herd of them—young calves and their mothers
and the great bulls, their antlers still small and in the velvet, for
every year these forest kings grow their crowns anew, having shed
the old. We drew the car cautiously to a stop and stepped out,
holding our breath lest we frighten away these wild things.
Quietly, quietly we stole toward them. And far from being timid,
the elk came ambling cheerfully up to us and nuzzled the boys'
outheld hands, plainly demanding something to eat! Hastily we

scrambled in our picnic basket and found them scraps. The monarchs of this primeval wilderness ate them as gratefully as a zoo elephant takes peanuts!

We learned that certain bands of the elk in the Park had discovered that on this one highway through the wilderness they could get a meal by begging instead of working for it. It is of course much healthier for them to stick to their natural diet of grasses, sedges, salmonberries, the bark of alder and willow, the big bracken fern, and the salal berries with a spicy taste. But their greedy friendliness gave us a chance to see them well.

And what a sight is the bull, standing five feet high at the shoulders, weighing seven hundred pounds and more! Later in the autumn, in the mating season, his antlers are full-grown, many-branched, and sharp as swords, carried up and back over his body, not curving forward like a deer's. He wears a dark thick mane like a fur piece around his deep throat with its big pouch that grows even bigger as the mating season comes on. Then, when a bull is challenged by another, the throat distends with splendid rage. Both creatures blow a hoarse bugle blast out of those swelling throats; they rear up on their hind legs and put their heads down to rip the deep mossy floor of the forest with their antlers. Each having warned the other of the fight to come, they advance, and the clash comes, antler against branching antler. As each tries to shove the other back, the horns scrape and rasp together like the trees overhead when a torrent of wind rubs bough on bough.

The victor of the combat inherits the whole herd of cows, for an elk bull has as many wives as a sultan. Six to twenty cows may belong to a single, antlered lord and master. The peaceful cows accept this as the ancient custom of their race and show

fight only in defense of their calves. These are born late the following spring. Then the mother elk is so proud of her new baby and
of herself for producing him that she too sometimes bugles like
the male—a single long shrill cry of wild maternal triumph. Hearing it, the other elk cows may come to cluster around and lick the
baby, for their warm instincts lead them to take an interest in one
another's young. Soon the little thing struggles to its feet and is
quickly pushed by its mother into the deepest concealment that
that forest offers, where his dappled coat makes him look like the
flicker of sun on shade over some old stump.

How secret and profound these woods, we found when we
ventured into them. The carpet of mosses is so deep above the
layers of ancient rotting wood on the forest floor that your footfall
is soundless. In ten minutes of walking, you will have put so many
trunks and boughs, head-high ferns and giant huckleberry bushes
between you and your starting place that you fear you are lost.
We called and found one another, and then we were still, listen-

ing to the deep, surf-like sigh of the canopy overhead, high and scented and shadowy now with twilight.

All at once there sounded through the forest a throbbing boom. It seemed to start far in the forest and come rolling toward us, and past us, only to bounce back in echo. *Boop, boop, boop-a-doop, boooo!* It sounded like a deep-throated yet somehow friendly ghost knocking on the big boles of the Douglas fir. But I knew what it was—the call of the sooty grouse. The cock birds have curious air sacs in their throats, and now in the mating season and all during the nesting season (it was June) the deeply folded and elastic skin over these sacs can be expanded into a yellow balloon. It is the rush of air into these sacs which makes the booming of the grouse. The boys soon got the hang of it; by filling their cheeks tight with air and then saying "Oomph!" in their throats, they imitated the grouse well enough to fool me.

That was a holiday we will remember always, for we felt we had found a little bit of America as God made it. This was unspoiled, aboriginal wilderness. Everything was made in the perfect balance that only Nature can keep. No invaders had come here, not a weed, not a rat, nor chirping English sparrow; nothing upset the balanced life that had been flowing on here since before the dawn of our history. If the elk, or the black-tailed deer, should grow too numerous for their own food supply, the mountain lions and bobcats which prey on them would soon grow numerous too and cut down the numbers of elk and deer to something the forest can support. Then, as the deer and elk fell off in numbers, the lions and wild cats would turn to other game or begin to decrease in numbers from lack of food supply. Even the forest trees and mosses, and the huge fungi on their trunks, are in balance also. The great trees give the shade that the mosses love. The mosses hold the soil from washing away under the torrential rains of the Olympic Peninsula. The fungi, always favored by rain, devour in their own way the fallen logs. Out of the rich mouldy earth, new trees spring up.

This is the balance of Nature—a harmony that is like a beautiful chord of music humming on forever. Only by respecting Nature, by taking no more of her bounty than she can afford to give and we actually need, can we keep the delicate balance from dipping down into destruction.

THE SHORE

Most of the world is water. That's a thing hard to believe, unless you are crossing the ocean. Then, as day after day goes by with nothing in sight all around the ship but endless tossing waves, you can easily understand that two thirds of this spinning globe are covered by its seas. And those deep, dark, cold unfriendly regions are full of a life of their own, strange and fierce and sometimes weirdly beautiful. Equally fascinating is the betwixt and between life of the shore.

Of all the seaside provinces to be found along the shores of America, my favorite is a small one just midway on the coast of California, near Monterey, and there is so much Nature to study there that I go back again and again. Sometimes this pine-clad tumble of rocks jutting out into rough water is wreathed in mys-

97

terious fog. Then on the salt cold wind there blows to me a chorus of deep, hoarse, snoring barks that mingle with the crash of waves. This noise is made by a herd of sea lions that love to sprawl and bask on the rocks out there at the end of the point.

On a clear mellow day such as comes most often in autumn to the Monterey peninsula, you see these great beasts lolling in comfort there in the sun or slithering off to wallow in the water. The cliffs of Point Lobos hold the sunshine like a cup so that you can settle down to watch the sea lions in comfort. You can see that the ones which have been sunning long enough to get dry are a dull, golden brown; the wet ones look darker. Most of them are the California sea lion, and if they look familiar it is because this is sometimes the animal you see in circuses balancing a ball on the end of his nose. But you will notice even bigger beasts in the herd out there on the rocks; these are Steller's sea lions, and some of them may be as much as thirteen feet long and weigh a ton. The enormous bulls snarl and snap at each other and sway their heads around as if looking for trouble. They are awkward enough as they flounder around on the rock using their fin-like feet, but once in the water they are easy and tireless. Yet baby sea lions have to be taught to swim! The mother takes them by the scruff of the neck as a dog carries her pup and plops them into the water; in two months they are swimmers as expert as she.

On another rock near by perch a lot of cormorants, dark birds

with snaky necks. (In China, a fisherman will tame a cormorant and put a ring around his long neck so that the bird, when it catches a big fish, cannot swallow it—the fisherman gets it instead!) Pelicans go flying by in a formation as regular as that of an airplane squadron. When this bird, more beak than bird, sees a fish he wants in the water below, he seems to put on his brakes in mid-air and plummets down in a steep dive.

Nearby stands a red-billed oyster catcher, and though I have watched him for hours, I have never seen him catch an oyster yet. He may have for companion a timid, brownish-gray bird called a wandering tattler, which sounds like the kind of person that goes around spreading gossip. But the tattler has never said a word to me, only poked silently about at the water's edge.

The greatest beast of all, on this coast, is not alive, yet it charges and roars. It is the never-ceasing surf itself. The ocean may look calm and smiling a little farther out, but like some monstrous animal profoundly breathing, it is forever sending in long rollers. As they reach the shallow water, the bottom of the wave begins to drag while the crest plunges toppling forward to smash on the rocks with the force of many tons. Splashing high up on the coast, it sends a shower of spray higher still that drenches the flowers on the cliff—sea thrift and sea daisies which can endure salt-water showers. That anything could live where the full force of the waves thunders down on it, seems incredible. Yet this is one of the most richly inhabited parts of the whole world.

And of all the organisms that flourish in the surf, the sea palms are the most surprising. They look like palms seen through the wrong end of a telescope, for they are only about a foot high. And of course they aren't truly palms, but a kind of seaweed, dusky olive in color. Unlike all other seaweeds they can stand up straight when out of water on their rubbery, resistant stalks, their foliage of long waving blades looking like a mad tangle of mermaid locks. As each breaker crashes down on them, they bend down to the rock; their green tresses struggle and writhe and disappear in the seething foam. Then when the wave draws back, the stalks right themselves again and seem to toss out their wet, shining tresses with a laugh, like a girl who has just dived happily through a breaker.

Yet if you pluck a sea palm from its rock and try to take it home, in a few hours it goes all soft and turns to a half-liquid mess. It

was life that gave it the strength to withstand the battering of the surf and even to rejoice in it.

Where tides rise high and then sink low, where the surf reaches far up the rocks one minute and leaves them dry the next, it is hard to say just what is ocean and what is land. Some marine life certainly creeps up the cliffs into what is called the splash zone. One such is the owl limpet, a seashell animal, sometimes the size of a silver dollar, that clings to the rocks with a fierce grip. But

it can relax its grip when it wants to and wander away looking for food; when it does so it leaves a sort of scar on the rock. And marine biologists tell us that a limpet returns to its own private scar; it knows it—don't ask me how—from every other limpet scar even if there are a thousand near by.

In the zone reached only by the high tides, you meet the first of the crabs. The porcelain crab can escape you even after you have grabbed him, by just parting with the leg you hold, which snaps off as easily as the handle of a porcelain cup. The cup cannot grow a new handle; the crab can, and easily does, grow new legs. The dainty black and white brittle-stars, too, can cast off the ray of their "stars." They dismember themselves right in your hand, but they haven't committed suicide. Quickly they will grow new "rays."

The hermit crabs of this zone get their name from their habit of living by themselves, each one in an empty shell of one of the sea snails. Little hermits crawl into little shells; soon outgrowing

them, they scurry around to find a bigger shell—one not too big, or they couldn't drag it and it wouldn't protect them. So they keep "moving house," like city apartment-dwellers who are forever vacating one dwelling, only to have somebody else move in after them.

Here, too, you may happen to see a small surf-loving snail with the grand-opera name of Thais and a role in ancient history. For, though its short spiral shell is only black and white, the living creature inside secretes, when dug out, a dye that will stain your fingers purple for a few hours. Merchants of the seaport of Tyre used to sell this dye all over the Mediterranean world, and Tyrian purple formed part of the wealth of that ancient city.

When the tide is low you can venture farther out always keeping a wary eye out for the occasional big wave. Here some animals swim boldly about in clear, enchanting tidal pools; others attach themselves firmly to exposed rocks; others, more cautious, hide

under rocks or beneath the masses of seaweed left limp by the receding waters.

This is the place to make acquaintance with sea anemones, an acquaintance that shouldn't include touching them with fingers or bare toes, for they can sting like a nettle leaf. True, these animal "flowers of the sea" only blossom out in full beauty when covered with water. When the tide is out, they close up and look dingy. Indeed, they cover themselves with bits of gravel, shell, or sand and appear at such moments as nothing but a squashy mass. If you tread on them, they send up bubbles and little geysers of water.

But if you have the luck to find them growing in a tidal pool, they may be expanded in all their beauty. Some are green, some red, some blue, and to my eye they look more like a dahlia than an anemone. Nor do they lead the gentle lives of flowers. Woe to the innocent little crab who comes within reach of their fiery tentacles that will drag him in to the hungry center of the anemone. The meal over, the anemone spews out the indigestible fragments of shell. But the creature seems to know the difference between a meal and an unfriendly poke. It you touch an open anemone with a stick, it closes up in the twinkling of an eye and sulks for a long time before it opens again.

Red, purple, and green are the sea urchins you will see here. This lowly animal is as prickly as a porcupine and no more minds the surf than do the sea palms. He tucks himself securely into holes in the rocks which he digs with his spines. No matter how hard the rock, a sea urchin can replace his worn-out prickles and drill on till he has a house. These spines are movable, too. If you prod him with a sharp bit of shell, the spines come together for protection. But when a starfish wants to make a dinner of the sea urchin, the spines move away in order to give play to some stinging hairs. These may discourage the starfish, but if he has persistence to nibble away one hair after another, the poor sea urchin will succumb in the end.

In the next lowest zone, farther in the sea, the little octopus lives and the abalone with his beautiful shell. Here dwell the masking crabs who cover themselves with seaweed in order to stalk up on their prey just as the Indians wore deer headdresses to creep up on the buffalo. And here collectors catch the pistol shrimps which snap their "fingers" with a sound like a boy's cap-pistol going off. This zone is too dangerous, most of the time, for you to enter, because the treacherous surf, even at low tide, may suddenly lift its white fangs. So here we have to leave the underworld of the ocean, a place more crowded with colorful and ruthless characters than the most lurid motion picture. But the naturalist remembers always that it is there—a life rich and beautiful in form, as marvelously adapted to surf and tide, to lightless and icy depths under terrible pressure, as ever life is to the land.

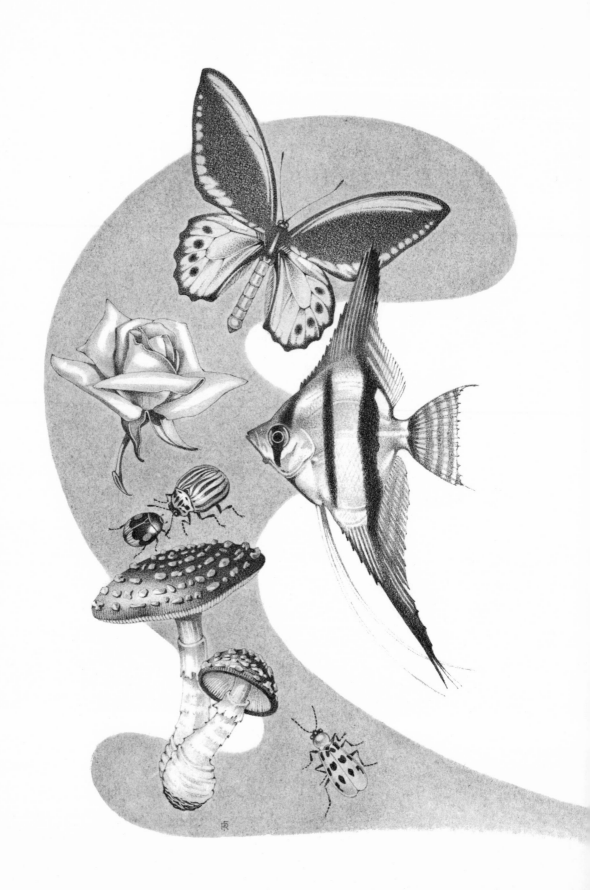

III.

THE

COLORS

OF

LIFE

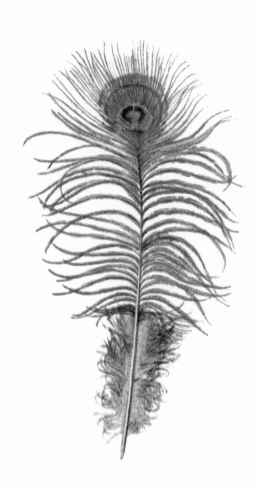

PIGMENTS AND PRISMS

A SMALL girl walking in the zoo with her mother saw for
the first time a peacock spreading its tail. "Oh, look,
Mommy!" she cried excitedly, "The chickens are in
flower!"

Flashing green and purple fires from the "eyes" on those high,
fanned-out feathers, the peacock is as breath-taking as it is boast-
ful. Small wonder that it has been carried, in domestication,
around the world from its original home at the foot of the Hima-
laya mountains. Through the ages its plumage has found a place
in throne room and pageant and procession. In the burial ship of
a viking chieftain, dug up in Norway a few years ago, among the
prized possessions laid away with that old seafarer was found a
single peacock feather. That viking lived in the Dark Ages (about

800 A.D.). Did he get his precious plume by barter with foreign traders? Certainly he found in it the same delight felt by the little girl at the zoo.

For we all rejoice in the endlessly varied hues of this highly colored world of ours. Its seas and sunsets, rocks and rivers are background to the flash and glow of life itself. In living things, color is produced two different ways. One is by pigment, the color that is right there in the leaf, or the flower, or the freckles on a boy's nose. The paints in a paintbox are pigments. But the colors that flash from a dewdrop, or a prism, are not. They are light broken upon into rainbow tints, prism colors. They do not lie within the object but are cast out by it in glitter, sheen, or iridescence.

The peacock can boast both kinds in his brilliant tail plumage. Some of the feathers contain pigment colors, and others have none, yet glisten vividly. That is because they are scratched with a minute crosshatching called striations, which act like prisms. As the bird struts haughtily about, these striations catch the light and break it flashing into violets, blues, and greens.

True pigment colors, however, are the rich, soft, restful greens that fill the summer scene. Then come the first fresh days of September with high blue skies and crows calling, and the leaves begin to change color. The touch of frost in the air has nothing to do with it for all those old fairy tales about Jack and his paintbox. Instead, it is the leaf itself that prepares its own end. It grows a row of brittle cells at the base of its twig, which gradually cut off the circulation of sap. With the loss of sap, the life goes out of the leaf, the vital green in it ebbs away, and there show forth yellow and red pigments. These have been in the leaf all along, but they were masked by the green.

Different chemicals in the leaves and the soil account for various shades that make the autumn glory of the foliage. So we have the reds and yellows of the maples like leaping bonfires down the street. Aspens up the mountain slopes are rivers of pure gold. Some oaks are golden, some glow ruby-red when the last warm sunshine filters through them. And through the woods runs a creeping fire of sumach, ruddy and smouldering. The whole high-hearted display is as American as our flag, for nowhere in the Old World does autumn come with such a shout of triumphant color.

Pigments alone account for the brilliance of some of our common butterflies like the sulphur-yellows. Others, like the great unearthly blue Morphos of South America, are colored by reason of their iridescence; still others are both pigmented and prismatic. If you ask to see beetles in a big museum, they will show you trays of them, sapphire blue, or metallic green, or deep violet, or bright green with crimson stripes, or rainbow-hued beetles—blue, green, yellow, violet, and red. The little goldsmith beetle (quite common in our country) looks as if hammered out by fairy workmen. If you have read "The Gold Bug" by Edgar Allan Poe, you will remember an insect that is not strictly a bug but really a beetle; some-

times it is dull yellow, and again it shines like burnished gold or even shimmers with mother-of-pearl tints. And yet, if you were to take the glittering wing-covers of some of the brightest of these beetles and grind them up to powder, you would have nothing but a pinch of gray dust. There was no real color, no pigment in them. It was all "done with mirrors," as the trick magicians say.

There's a lot of this glitter in the insect world. Though the honeybee is a modest creature, some of the wild bees and their relatives, the wasps, flash through the air in dazzling purples and greens, or velvety black with tigerish yellow stripes. Some have a green thorax (the part which roughly corresponds to your chest) and ruby abdomen, or a blue thorax and black abdomen. Even some ants, in tropical lands, are red and blue and green.

As for the fishes, anyone who has ever kept an aquarium knows what prisms their scales can be. The commonest goldfish are shimmering marvels, used to them though we are, and the rarer species are fantastic. The male paradise fish—which watches so carefully over his nest of bubbles—has shimmering cross-stripes of red and green. The danios are striped lengthwise, blue and gold, while the Mexican swordtail is opalescent. You have seen this same lovely lustre if you have ever landed a rainbow trout from some swift-running stream. Its fleeting colors roll and melt and change as it struggles its last, like the colors of an opal ring turned on the finger.

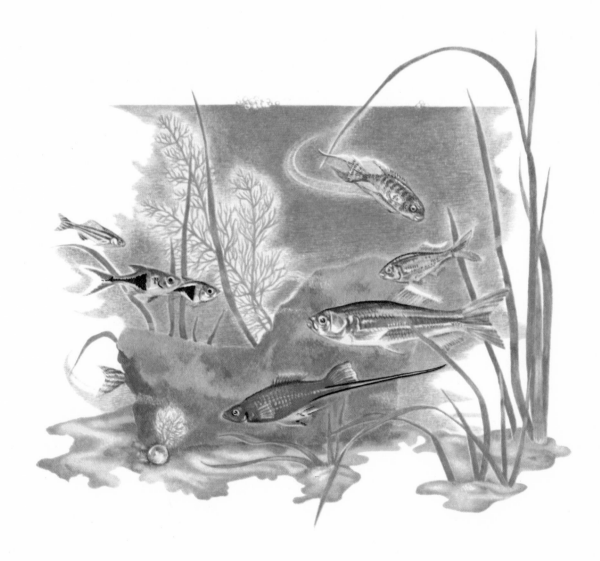

But no prism colors in Nature flash such airy fires as the feathers of the hummingbird. Here in my California garden on any summer day I can see the black-chinned hummingbird dart ruby lights from his throat feathers. Or up in the hills I find another kind with a black throat that suddenly shows an exquisite violet when he is courting his mate. Of hummingbirds, there are in the wide world 650 species. I have a friend who has personally collected 588 of these, in the lands where they are at home. This collection, the delicately stuffed little bodies all laid neatly in drawers, is like a gathering of princely gems. One after another he laid these fairy-light specimens in my hand, and I would gently tilt it so that the plumage shot forth those jewel tones—prism color, rainbow color. It was visible magic, if there is any such on earth.

And if beauty is not a kind of magic, what is? Beauty is a part of life, a wonderful overflow from it, a precious extra. For not everything in the great scheme of the living world serves a useful end. The autumn splendor of the woods, like a shout of praise, is of no real use to the tree. It is we who rejoice in it, walking under it through the bright rustle of fallen leaves on the way to work or school.

COLORS TO SHOW OFF

COLOR in Nature is not just a means of concealment, or a sheer, unmeaning extravagance of beauty. Sometimes it is a gay bid for feminine attention. It is famous that the cock bird, or male, of most species wears brighter plumage than his mate. And there are some animals which put on a special show to impress her at the time of courting.

In the dry, bright, sunburnt mountains of our Southwest lives a lizard whose colors are so brilliant, whose antics are so comical, that it is hard to remember he belongs to the class of the reptiles, usually so subtle and solemn. He is called the collared lizard because around his neck he wears skin with black and white bands, elegant as a man dressed for a formal dinner in "black tie." His head is orange, so is his throat, and his body is handsomely banded and speckled. Far from melting into the rock slide or stony crag where he likes to bask, this creature catches the astonished eye at once. And in the mating season, just in case he doesn't impress the lady lizard enough in his everyday clothes, he can suddenly swell out his dewlap, or throat pouch of elastic skin, so that it looks like a great jewel on his shirt front glowing sapphire or emerald.

She, on the contrary, wears no such brilliant hues, but he is less interested in her looks than in having her notice his. So when he goes a-wooing he performs antics designed to display his splendor. He flattens his body sideways and rears on his hind legs and throws out his chest. He prances and minces and sidles around, all the time bobbing his head as if to persuade the female to say "Yes, yes!" She may, however, play hard to get. Her way of saying "No, no!" is to hump her back and hop stiffly away, with her tail (instead of her nose) in the air. But a female's "no" is not always final, and if the determined suitor gives chase, there is often a wild, romping run-around that looks as much fun as a square dance.

It is not only the female lizards that take notice of the brilliance of a courting male. It is by that color that other males too—sometimes with extreme displeasure—recognize a rival. When they meet they fall to fighting, rearing, and throwing out their dewlaps. Often the whole body becomes suffused with color. They positively light up with jealousy.

Some fish, cold-blooded though they are, also color up with the excitements of this season of their lives. At the pet store you may buy jewelfish, a toy fish from African rivers that thrives well in an aquarium. At ordinary times he is not especially handsome; as a father, he is a model parent who guards the eggs, fanning them continuously to keep a supply of fresh, oxygen-rich water stirring over them. And since the babies, for the first few days, cannot swim, he fans out a little hollow for them in the sand and then stands guard over them till they are ready to navigate; even then he accompanies their school for a while.

But in the breeding season his body becomes a brilliant red, glittering with spots of emerald along his flanks, fins, and tail. These spots are the jewelry of the jewelfish, adornment to attract a mate. If another male, equally gaudy, comes along to interfere, a furious fight ensues. The beaten rival not only seeks safety in flight, but his jewels lose their lustre, his brilliant color fades. Ashamed, he slinks into hiding. The winner, however, seems to glister more brightly than ever, and he now expects to be accepted by the female, who must have been thoroughly impressed and dazzled.

Beauty of plumage has brought some species of our birds nearly to extinction. The snowy egrets used to be slaughtered for the glistering loveliness of the plumes worn only at breeding time, until the Audubon Society came to their rescue, and a law was passed forbidding the sale of these plumes, once fashionable on ladies' hats. The roseate spoonbill, a big bird of the Florida swamps, as pink as a tropical sunset, also nearly paid for his loveliness with his life. Today the conservation society named for the greatest of all bird painters, John James Audubon, is protecting the spoonbills and many another rare species.

But in New Guinea, the biggest and least explored islands in the Pacific, there was no such policing force to save the birds-of-paradise. For centuries men have been killing these enchanting creatures for the splendor of the males' plumage. This is probably the most gorgeous and fantastic group of birds in all the world. One species may wear iridescent plumage of every tint in the rainbow and be crowned by plumes twice as long as the body and even more brilliant. Another may have a tail drawn out fine as wire twisted into elaborate shape. Other species may wear glistering feather capes or sets of extra plumes that can be lifted, during courtship, so that the male seems four-winged, like some huge, gorgeous butterfly.

No wonder that these living marvels were hunted through the rain forests by the natives and sold by them to Arab and European traders. In order to pack the exquisite corpses more tightly for shipping, the merchants often cut off the feet. In this way they arrived in Europe for sale, and so grew up the belief that the birds-of-paradise had no feet and spent their entire lives on the wing, supping only on the nectar of flowers!

Today the sale of their plumes has been stopped in civilized countries by law. But the birds are still so rare, even high in the mountain jungles of New Guinea, that few white men have ever

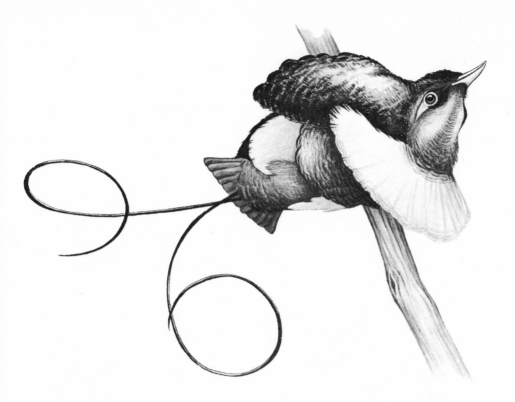

seen them at their courting. One scientist, Dr. A. L. Rand of the
American Museum of Natural History in New York, traveled all
the way out to that tropical wilderness just for this. From a hide-
out of palm leaves, he watched the courting of the bird-of-paradise
known as the magnificent—a creature worthy of his name, with
his emerald-green bib, pale yellow ruff, puff of deep crimson on
the back, wings that showed bright yellow when raised, and a tail
ending in two long central pinions like steel-blue coiled springs.
The bird cleared a little dance floor or display ground on the forest
earth, and when the female came he performed for her. He pulsed
out his shimmering green-blue breastplate till it rose in points on
each side of his head; he could roll its feathers till they sparkled
like gems on a queen's fingers. As the plainly dressed female
slipped coyly around a tree in the center of the dance floor, he
turned too, always keeping his splendor before her. Now suddenly

he threw up his fantastic tail and the ruff behind his head, holding this spread like a golden fan that trembles in tense fingers. As if irresistibly drawn by the display the shy brown bird hopped closer to her chosen mate.

And yet not all the animals, by any means, see the world in technicolor. Of the mammals, only the primates—by which the naturalist means the monkeys and their kin—are able to see color at all. The rest are color-blind. The tiger, gorgeous in black-striped yellow, is to another tiger just a pattern of in-between shades of gray and black. His eyes are quick for movement, his nose for scent, his ears for sound. But the radiant variations of the multi-colored world bring him no messages. The monkey kind, on the other hand, seem to admire each other for any adornments of color with which they may be created. And on the mandrills and baboons Nature paints these in clownish places!

COLORS TO HIDE IN

A NAVY ship painted over in fantastic camouflage catches the eye at once as it lies near by in the calm blue harbor. It looks like an especially easy mark for enemy guns. But out at sea, in the tossing waters that change from green to blue to gray under the scudding clouds, a camouflaged vessel may glide unnoticed where a plain gray craft would be spotted at once. Or, if it is observed, at least its size and shape are harder to distinguish. So confusing is that painted pattern that sometimes the enemy cannot even make out which end is bow and which is stern, or whether the ship is fleeing away or dashing forward to attack.

War and its dangers challenge man to invent ever new methods of defense. But camouflage is old, older than man himself. It occurs over and over in Nature and not in tropic jungles only, and

127

the depths of the sea, but in our American woods and fields, even in the bushes around your house.

The bobwhite is a friendly bird, that likes to sit right up on the top rail in a thickety fence row and whistle his name *Bob-WHITE! Bob-bob-WHITE!* That cheery call tells the whole world where and who he is. But it's a different story when these little quail are hiding from the hunter. The man with the gun may be nearly upon them before he touches off a bobwhite "bomb."

For it is almost impossible to see a bobwhite covey on the forest floor before it has seen you. The mottled pattern of their plumage so breaks up the outlines of the birds that they blend right into the leaves. There may be half a dozen of them hiding so together, their tails pointing toward the center of the circle, their heads looking out in all directions. There they lie, aware of your every footfall

through the woods, perfectly still, sharply alert. Then, when your next step is almost upon them—the bomb explodes! With a whir of wings, they burst away, each to a different point of the compass. And while you are getting over your startlement and gathering your wits, the birds have dropped quietly down into the underbrush and are scurrying for deeper cover.

In my garden, in some low juniper bushes beside the path, a ring-necked pheasant last year chose to make her nest. Her mate is a handsome show-off. With red patches on his face like a circus clown, with his iridescent greenish, purplish neck feathers and his long, dramatically dragging tail, he is certain to be noticed and admired the moment he appears. But the female pheasant dresses with modesty and caution. Her back, all speckled and marked with wavy lines like a hundred little flounces, blended so well with the dapple of shade and the pattern of juniper that I never knew she was there for days. Even my dog, a bird dog too, trotted down the path many a time without suspecting her presence. Then one day I came to prune the junipers and found myself looking straight into the dark jewels of her eyes. She just sat quietly on those precious eggs of hers, and her unwinking gaze seemed to plead with me, as if to say, "Yes, you've found me out, but you won't tell the dog, will you?" And of course I didn't tell the dog, and I didn't prune the bush or even look her way for some time. When at last I ventured to peep again, I found only a little clutch of empty eggshells. The chicks had hatched, and the mother bird must have led them quietly away.

Protective coloring is the best defense of many a gentle animal. Merciless are the enemies of the deer, and helpless their big-eyed, stiff-legged young. But the dappled coat of the fawn looks so like the spots of sun and shadow on the forest floor that unless the

little creature moves he is almost invisible. And fawns are so obedient that they will scarcely twitch an eyelid as they lie where their mothers put them. Even at your approach, the fawn will not stir or startle. Meanwhile, the doe is likely to draw your attention to herself, moving off gradually, always away from her child. If still you go closer to the fawn, it remains motionless, but you had best not touch it or try to pick it up. That gentle mother can attack quick as a flash with hooves as sharp as razors.

Just as woodland creatures so often resemble the forest floor, so desert animals are apt to be desert-colored—dust-gray, pebbly mottled, or rock-rough like the horned toad or lizard. There is nothing harder to see clearly than those distance-keeping antelopes, those sly kit foxes, those kangaroo rats camouflaged by their subdued colors against all detection—until they move. Even then you cannot be sure that it was not the sandy dust which stirred and fled before the wind or a bit of tumbleweed doing somersaults.

But as usual it is the insects that carry to fantastic lengths this foolery of concealment. Their disguises go beyond the camouflage of color and pattern, and take imitative shapes. In our own woods are many kinds of little green leafhoppers, or "brownie bugs," that pass for half-expanded leaf buds on the twig, look like thorns, or

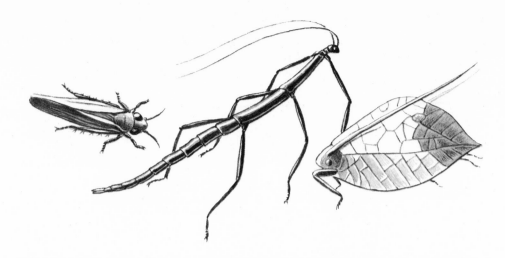

even hooked seeds. None is a better mimic than the insect called the walking-stick. Staring right at it, you will think it is just a twig growing with other twigs on the bough of bush or tree. This mimicry is a three-way trick. First, you are deceived by the insect's outline, rigid and skeleton-thin, while some of the creature's organs take on the look of closed buds. Then, there is the disguise of its color—greenish or brownish, yellowish or grayish or dull ruddy. And last, the creature hides in absolute stillness and at an angle just like that of a twig growing from a branch. So patiently "lifeless" will it remain that you have to touch it before it will unlimber its absurdly stiff and angular legs and make off with an air of offended dignity, like somebody at a costume party whose disguise has been spoiled.

The tricks of the tropical leaf insects are more startling yet. Attaching themselves to trees, these extremely flattened creatures spread their wings, which are not only leaf-green but carry a pattern just like the midrib and veins and veinlets of a leaf. Even the insect's legs have flat, leaf-like projections to deceive your eye. And to fool you and their natural enemies further, their eggs look exactly like little round seeds.

You have heard the expression "a wolf in sheep's clothing"

meaning a villain wearing a look of innocence. Some creatures, in reverse, are sheep in wolves' clothing; they find safety in looking dangerous. A defenseless African fly mimics a stinging carpenter bee almost exactly, down to every detail of color and form. Certain African butterflies, quite harmless to any bird that may eat them, look just like the poisonous kind, and naturalists have proved by experiments that the birds do leave them strictly alone. In Britain one naturalist discovered, living in ant nests, twenty-eight species of creatures *not* ants but looking so like them that no scientist, till then, had realized they were not. Not that the ants themselves could have been fooled, for ants know their own kind by smell. But doubtless all the many creatures that leave ants alone because of their bites and stings and burning acid taste also left unmolested the mimics sheltering there.

The idea of camouflage is so fascinating that one can get carried away by it—out of the realm of reality into nonsense. There's an old joke about the chameleon that had a nervous breakdown when put on Scotch plaid! True that this little lizard can slowly change color to match its background, but it also colors up the way a girl may blush, due to emotions whether of fear or anger or to changes in temperature and light. And, though he never meant to be funny, one artist naturalist has suggested that the beautiful pink plumage of the flamingoes helps to make them harder to see when flying against the sunset. But what's a poor flamingo to do when the sun isn't setting or rising?

FLYING COLORS

SOMETIMES a lucky passenger is allowed to visit the cockpit of a big airliner. There you can see the pilot and his crew as they take the great ship, sometimes seventy tons in weight, through the boundless seas of air. You can watch them at the controls, puzzle over the many mysterious gauges and dials, and wonder at the radio signals coming in with news of weather conditions. And you realize that the sky is a whole new dimension with traffic lanes and communication channels and a geography all its own.

Now imagine that instead of an airplane you could enter the head of a honeybee. Call it a beeplane. If you could see as the bee sees, "tune in" with the equipment in her brain, you would scarcely recognize the vacant lot next door to you, as she buzzes the weed-

133

tops. You wouldn't even hear that buzz, for bees have no ears, no organ of any sort with which to listen. On the other hand, the antennas of the beeplane pick up all sorts of messages, not of sound but of scent. From the white clover in the grass and the sweet melilot along the ditch come waves of perfume, and from the garden across the street other flower odors irresistibly summon the beeplane toward them.

As it flies in "on the beam" of the flowers' scents, their colors flash up before the cockpit windows, as you might call the bee's five eyes. But through these you would perceive the red flowers, and probably also the green leaves, only as shades of gray, for the honeybee is color-blind to red and green, just as some humans are. The bee, however, sees not only orange and yellow, blue and violet, but other hues that the human eye cannot behold. These are the ultraviolet tints, those waves in the rainbow color-band that lie beyond the visible violet. We know they are there although we cannot perceive them, for they are the rays that give us the tan and the burn in sunlight. Some photographic film can pick up this ultraviolet color, but it only shows dark in the picture. So on such film a picture of black-eyed susans makes it clear that their yellow rays are tipped with ultraviolet color although in the photograph this merely appears black. But to bees it is an attractive color for which they show marked preference.

And they are well aware not only of the many perfumes and tints of flowers but of their various shapes. Experiments with paper flowers have proved that bees remember the forms of the different kinds of blossoms that yield them nectar for their honey-making. So, as the beeplane zooms down over the garden bed, this happy hunting ground looks like a fairyland to you in the bee-brain cockpit. The head of an iris rises like a purple palace. A yellow tulip

is a crater filled with sunlight, and from the base of those huge painted petals lifts the geometric mechanism of its reproductive parts. And where a willow hangs its catkins over the garden pool, each tassel is a swinging pagoda from which a million golden balls drift away on every breath of breeze. That pollen the bees use in making bee-bread for their babies.

Now the beeplane descends to alight. And it is notable that most of the flowers visited by bees offer some sort of landing field whether hanging lip or shelving petals or level rays like a daisy's. For a bee cannot like a hummingbird or sphinx moth hover in the air before a flower while it sips the nectar; it must have its weight supported. An inviting spot for a bee to alight is the pouting lower lip of a snapdragon. As the bee crawls up it, the lip, depressed like

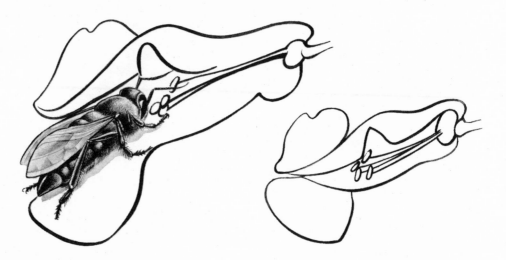

a pedal by her weight, sags. The bee walks in, to get her share of nectar and do her part in pollinating the flower, and the dragon's lower jaw snaps softly shut. When she is ready to leave, mistress bee backs out; again her weight unlocks the trap door, and she flies away as the dragon snaps shut again.

Honeybees have a systematic habit that is important to the successful fertilization of flowers. All the members of a given hive are apt to visit but one kind of flower at a time, usually the most nectar-full and sweetly perfumed of the moment. In this way they carry the pollen from the male flowers to the one right kind of female flowers. And flowers, of course, can only be fertilized by their own kind of pollen.

Some flowers, though, are literally beyond the honeybee, which has a tongue too short to reach into such places as the deep spurs in which the columbine secretes its nectar. She has to leave flowers like that to the butterfly, whose long unrolling tongue plunges easily into them. A fickle, light-headed nectar-sipper, however, is the butterfly, for it goes idly from one kind of flower to another, getting dusted with scores of different pollens. Its preference is often for those red flowers the bee cannot see at all. It adores the brilliant orange-red butterfly-weed of the open meadows, and any

summer day that you come on this plant, you'll find a butterfly turning around on the head of it, delicately guzzling.

Hummingbirds, too, love red flowers with deep spurs full of nectar. A favorite of the ruby-throated hummingbird is the coral honeysuckle which used to grow around the porch when I was a boy and lived down South. At almost any daytime hour I could see a hummingbird there, hovering on the air in front of the flower, visiting one blossom after another, quick with its long tongue as the jab of a doctor's needle, invisibly but surely transferring pollen from one bloom to the next. These swift-tempered tiny birds can be attracted too by a vial of sugared water framed at its lips with little artificial petals, preferably red. I know a woman, unable to leave her room, who set such pretty bait in the vines at her window and had hummers visiting her all summer long.

And the colorless flowers, the white ones that gleam and breathe most sweetly in the dusk—what creature comes to them? The moths, of course, that emerge only in the twilight. It is then that the pale flowers show best. The evening catchfly, which you will see around vacant lots and the edges of gardens, opens its flowers only when the sun goes down and the moths come out. Now it sends forth on the cooling air a scent not very strong to our blunted sense of smell but leading the perfume-loving, nectar-banqueting, long-tongued moths silently to it. By sunrise of the next day the moth is gone, the bloom is closed—and the flower's mating all secretly and perfectly accomplished.

IV.

THE

FORMS

OF

LIFE

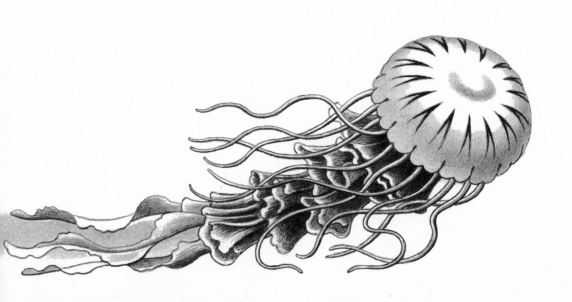

FORM AND FUNCTION

Tiger, tiger, burning bright
In the forests of the night,
What immortal hand or eye
Could frame thy fearful symmetry?

A NATURALIST might answer the poet Blake by saying that life has given form to everything living, tigers and turtles, banana trees and burdocks. Nothing in living Nature is formless, aimless, shapeless, as the wind is shapeless, as the mist is formless, as the driven dust is aimless. And in the forms of life are found two kinds of symmetry.

One is very simple and belongs to many of the simplest kinds of animal, like starfish, sand dollars, and sea anemones. This is radial

symmetry, which is that of a wheel. Anywhere you divide it down the middle, the two equal sides match identically. A great many flowers also are made on this plan. A glance at a daisy shows you its radial symmetry, which can be found, if you look for it, in a water lily or a wild rose too.

The tiger's symmetry is the two-sided kind called bilateral (*bi* meaning "two" and *lateral* meaning "sided"). You and I are organized bilaterally, and very convenient we find it. If either of us were divided right down the middle from top to toe, there would be an

eye, an ear, a nostril, an arm, a leg, on each side. Each side would exactly match the other, but in reverse—just the way our feet are mates. This is, when you stop to think of it, a very neat way to be arranged. At any rate, a vast number of creatures work on this two-sided plan—all insects, all mammals, all birds, fishes, reptiles, crabs, lobsters. To say nothing of many flowers—snapdragon, cardinal-flower, trumpet-creeper, for instance, and all the orchids, ten thousand species of them, each with its own fantastical and elaborate shape, every one on the bilateral plan.

Two-sided symmetry is the form in which all the higher creatures are organized—those that lead complex lives and have alert nervous systems and definite brains. This appears to be the best scheme Nature could find on which to arrange together such a lot of organs as eyes to see with, ears to hear with, wings to fly with, or lungs or gills to breathe with. Some of the animals, it is true, get along with very simple organs. But if they haven't legs, they usually have something that enables them to swim or creep or fly. If they haven't mouths, they have some way of wrapping themselves around a morsel of food. If they lack eyes, they will have, at least, some sensitivity and response to light and darkness. Plants, too, have organs such as roots, or the like, foliage of some kind, and if they have not all got the complicated organs that make up a flower, they have some system of reproduction.

And each living collection of organs, whether arranged by radial or bilateral symmetry, is (to use the naturalist's favorite word) an organism. If such things are too tiny to see without a microscope, he calls them micro-organisms.

Of all the million different kinds of living things, with their million different shapes, some of the loveliest are found among these primitive, ancient, simple plants and animals which are all but invisible. But put these micro-organisms under the lens, and the variety and beauty of their form is dazzling. They gleam with a splendor like that of crown jewels; for fragile delicacy they surpass Venetian glass. Indeed, their walls are made of silicon, which is an important part of glass, yet they float in water and live unbroken in rough seas. Only when their brief life span is over, does the little glass skeleton sink to the bottom.

Accumulating down there for millions of years, these micro-organisms form a deep, slithery ooze on the ocean floor. The layers

of ooze are named by scientists for the kind of micro-organism most abundant in it. When you roll these names on your tongue, they have an ogre-ish flavor. So if you want to scare somebody, turn out the lights and in a spooky voice recite the names of the four great ocean oozes, like this:

The Foraminiferan Ooze
The Radiolarian Ooze
The Diatomaceous Ooze!
The Globigerina Ooze!!

By this time your victim should be oozing terror. Turn on the lights and explain to him that this lesson in oceanography was merely to make the point that even in the mud at the bottom of the sea there are forms of life, if you care to go down and look for them.

Now, following the forms of life up from the oozy ocean floor

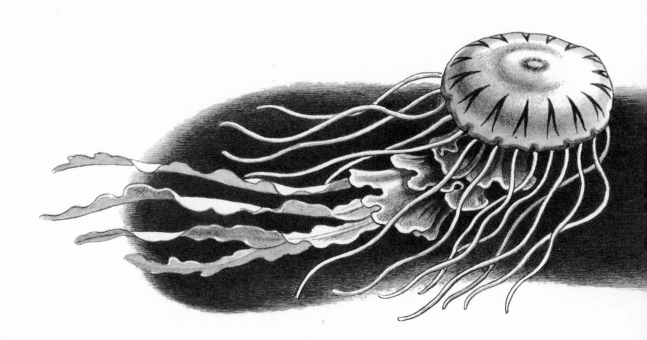

to the surface of the sea where the dolphins play, and all the way
up into rivers to the tinkling mountain brooks, let's have a look at
some of the aquatic animals and see how they are built to swim—
or not to swim.

Queerly enough, many creatures that live in the water can't
swim at all! Swimming requires a very complicated organization,
usually with bilateral symmetry. The lowly micro-organisms are
hard enough put to it just to keep from sinking! Other animals remain afloat by reason of a flattened out body, or they are helped
by feathery tails, or feather "feet," or wing-like projections from
the body. These are common anti-sinking devices to be found
among the larvae, or ungrown stages, of many sea worms, sea
snails, fishes, starfishes, sea urchins, and shellfish.

The ocean's bell-shaped creatures, like the jellyfish, are naturally buoyant because of their form; they can make progress of a
sort by wavering their tentacles and mantles. The devilish-looking,
big flat creature called a ray, which you often see in large aquar-

iums, ripples the soft thin sides of his mantle, and so seems to wave himself along the floor of the tank. This looks like a poor enough way to get through the water, but the ray has to do the best he can with the way he is made. And so do you, though you may be able to "swim like a fish," as people say.

For of course no human being *can* swim anything like a fish, since our form is quite un-fishlike. We use our jointed arms and legs like oars. The big solemn sea turtles do the same; the rollicking seals also swim by using their flippers. And penguins, those antarctic birds whose wings are so short they cannot fly, find these so useful in the water, together with their webbed feet, that they lead lives more fishy than bird-like.

But nothing can equal the marvelous swimming organization of a fish. Powerful muscles undulate its body while the tail acts as a rudder, enabling the fish to dart to one side or to reverse in a way

the best trick-swimmer among us can never do. Yet not all fishes
are built alike. There are flat fishes and round fishes. Why? Because they are formed to live in very different kinds of water. The
flat-fish type—flat as a pancake standing on edge—is the kind you
see most commonly in pet store aquariums. Such fish display beautiful coloration on their flat sides, and look exquisitely graceful
sailing through the water, but they are really weak swimmers.
They are safe enough in an aquarium or in sluggish rivers, in calm
waters protected from surf by coral reefs, in lakes or in the motionless depths of the sea. But if one of these pretty flat creatures were
caught in the churning rapids of a great river or in the merciless
pounding surf, it would be spun sideways and round and round,
knocked flat, and soon knocked out.

Quite the opposite is the shape common to the fish of rushing

waters. They are built for strength and endurance, not grace. Some, like the miller's-thumb, well named from its thumb-like shape, are flattened not sideways but top-and-bottom, so they are broader than high and practically flat-bottomed—like a scow or sturdy barge. Round-bottomed, like a dory meant for heavy seas, are the roach and even the common minnow. The body of the steelhead trout is a masterpiece of naval construction. At once muscular and stoutly built, the steelhead leaps out of water and leaps again and again, climbing up the thundering falls of the Columbia River on the way to its spawning ground.

Fishes built for speed are streamlined. Not a single projection of any sort offers resistance to the water in the body of that champion swimmer, the blue shark. The swift mackerel even has special slots in the body into which the fins can be folded back when not in use. Seals and whales are similarly streamlined for fast and tireless swimming.

So an animal—or a plant—functions according to its form. It is organized for just the life it lives. And each organ in its organization seems to be fitted to do its own job. We could trace, through the animal kingdom, the power to fly, the power to climb, the power to see with all the many different sorts of eyes that animals have. But a certain wonderment would always remain. We would always be asking ourselves whether creatures developed these marvelous organs as they adapted themselves to different conditions, or whether the animals "got that way" first and then found the spot in the world where their powers could be used to greatest advantage? Which came first—form or function?

I don't know the answer. Wiser men than I don't know it either. And when you find a puzzle to which nobody knows the complete solution, you have something worth thinking and *thinking* about!

SHADE AND SUN

THE beauty of shape in leaves is endless. Here's a glossy mitten-shaped leaf—that's sassafras. This one that looks as though somebody had taken a bite out of the tip comes from a tulip tree. This, rather like a five-pointed star, is a sweet-gum leaf, and here's one divided in three parts—don't touch it! If you remember the old rhyme, "leaves three, let it be," you'll suspect it is poison ivy.

Not only do the different shapes of leaves tell you what kind of a tree or other plant they came from, but the one kind of shape they have in common is highly significant. Leaves are almost all flat, and that, when you come to think of it, is immensely important. A flag only reaches its full purpose and meaning when it is lifted by the breeze and flung out, snapping, to show its colors.

Only when you want to put it away do you furl a banner up as a leaf is furled and stored in bud. So each year the woods hang out their opened foliage once more, tiny banners spreading on the summer wind the triumphant colors of life.

And each leaf has two sides, an upper and a lower. That's important too, once you find out why. Counting both sides of the leaf, a fine old street tree may have altogether an acre of leaf surface. And that great spread-out green leafiness, tranquil and thoughtless though it is, performs some of the major work of the world.

Take a leaf and look at it. You'll notice that the upper surface usually is a little different from the underside. It is apt to be a deeper green. That green pigment in the leaf is chlorophyll, and it has the almost magical power of capturing the sunlight and using its energy. With this sun-power, the leaf silently performs a very complicated work that naturalists call photosynthesis. In this, the air the leaf breathes and the water it has drawn up from the plant's roots, are recombined into sugars and starches, which are the growing plant's food. So a tree in full sunlight is like a great busy factory but one which makes no roar or clatter and gives out no disagreeable smells. Indeed, the leaves are making our air more pleasant. For while their upper surfaces are catching the sunlight and working with it, the undersides are breathing through the many very tiny pores in them. They give out, at least by day, more oxygen than they use, and moisture also evaporates at these pores, and so all our atmosphere is refreshed by the great green mills of the world's foliage.

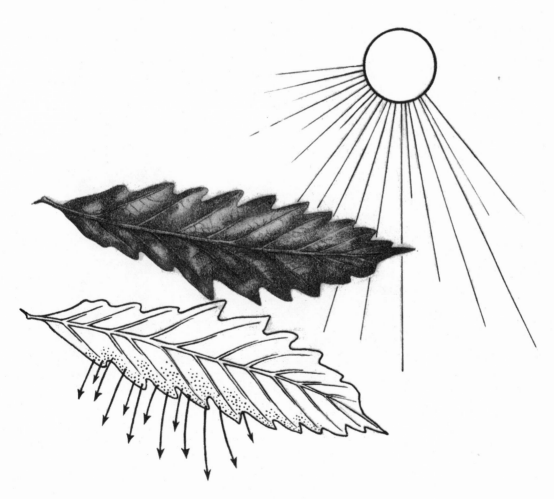

So you see what a lot hinges on such a simple fact as that leaves
are flat. Speaking of hinges, did you ever notice how the leaf of
an aspen or cottonwood is hung on the tree? Its flattened leafstalk
is set at right angles to the blade itself. And that's the answer to
one question asked at the beginning of this book—why do the
aspen leaves turn with a rustle and twinkle when no other leaves
stir? Like a swinging door on a two-way hinge, their leaves move
at every draft, and a breeze sets them pattering like rain, rustling
like silken skirts, whispering like boys in the back row at school.

A deeper voice that always seems to hush the listener is that of
the pines in the wind. The needles of a pine are leaves, of course,
not flat ones but shaped as though tightly rolled. This fits the tree
to live in dry places, for with less leaf surface there is less evapora-
tion of precious water. Other plants are shaped for a successful
life right in the water, such as the eelgrass which grows in lakes
in long, ribbony, wavy blades. Water lilies have leaves of the best
possible shape for floating on the surface; the Victoria water lily,
a favorite in city park ponds, has leaves turned up all around the
edge. A very small girl can actually sit on one of these great floating
leaves, her weight so well distributed over its broad expanse that
she remains high and dry on her lily pad just like a frog.

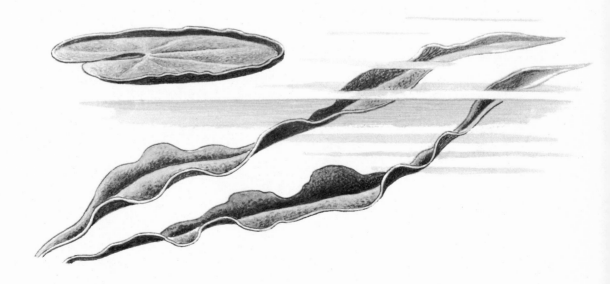

Leaves that grow deep in the shade are apt to be split up into separate, airy, lacy parts, like the trembling maidenhair fern. Others, in the fierce light and heat, wind and drought of the desert, expose as little surface as possible to such harsh conditions and

are no more than narrow blades. The leaves of some yuccas are like that and curl up at the ends into a sword-like point, so that, on the beaches of Florida, they are called Spanish bayonets.

Many a leaf has come to mean, to those who love it best, a spe-

cial place, a special pride. That of the sugar maple is the official symbol of Canada. The three-leaved clover called shamrock is the chosen emblem of Ireland. A branch of the olive tree has stood for peace since antiquity; the ancient Roman returning from his wars found peace at last in the olive groves of his countryside, where the soft green leaves show silver undersides in the wind. One tree, the ginkgo, treasured for thousands of years in the Buddhist temples where it grew, is now common as a street tree in our American cities. Sometimes in autumn you may see its leaf fallen on the pavement and pick it up to admire; a rich yellow, with its principal veins all running out from the base, it is a tiny golden fan from far Japan.

The more leaf shapes you can recognize, the more you will find that friends are lining the streets or roads you walk. Trees are living friends just as much as humans are, and each leaf of every tree, in fact, has a birth, childhood, prime of life, and death. This year's leaves got their start last year when the tiny buds were formed. Inside the bud a perfect baby leaf was curled or folded, and in this hidden way it was carried over winter for about nine months. Then, at the rising of sap and the warmth of spring, the buds swelled up and up till the infant blade burst its scales and unfurled into the early sunshine. There follows a period of rapid growth like that of human childhood. In summer, leaves, at fullest spread, do most of their work. At last they fade and fall, to be dissolved by the rains to a silvery skeleton that shows only a ghostly tracery of the system of veins. The wind of winter sweeps these

ghost leaves, whispering, across the streets, the lawns, the forest floors, till it is time for them to decay and so go back to earth. As rich leaf mold, they nourish other flowers, other leaves that in their turn have their hour, like us, in the light.

NAMES AND SYSTEM

ANYBODY can come to recognize the flowers common around his home region—the local flora, as naturalists say. And, if you don't already know them, you can easily master the names of the birds you most frequently see. For at this time of your life you learn most swiftly and remember most surely both what you see and what you read in books. If you want to find out how to identify birds and flowers, trees and insects, the shelves of the bookstores and libraries are crowded with books to help you, filled with fine pictures, clear descriptions, and keys to classification.

But it was not always so. Two hundred years ago natural history was just a welter of unassorted information freely sprinkled with *mis*information. As for the names of things, some beasts,

birds, and plants went by as many as five, ten, or twenty different names. And thousands of animals and plants had never been named at all—at least not in any European language, for they came from the farthest corners of the earth. The Dutch East India Company, which had trading posts in South Africa and the Spice Islands, was sending home to scholars in Holland specimens of tropical orchids and rare timbers like sandalwood and ebony, of bird-of-paradise and parrots and monkeys, never seen before. The far-ranging British were collecting curiosities in North America and India. Russian scientists were exploring unknown Siberia; the Spanish and Portuguese were bringing surprising treasures of

Nature out of South and Central America, and in Paris the museums and zoos were a perfect Noah's ark of queer "critters."

How to make order of all this? How to name, and describe, and classify all these new and strange and different specimens so that natural history could have some system in it? Many learned men were weltering along in the sea of confusion, each trying to steer the ark in his own way. What was needed was a genius to take the helm and steer a true course.

That genius was born in a one-room cottage deep in the Swedish

countryside in 1707. His name was Carl Linnaeus (pronounce it lin-*nee*-us). His father was a Lutheran minister who had no more money than you would expect of a country parson. But he had more education than the simple peasants of his church. He knew some Latin, and in those days Latin was not yet a wholly dead tongue applied to schoolboys as mental discipline. It was then used as a handy international language in which physicians, lawyers, diplomats, scientists, churchmen, and other educated people wrote to each other all over Europe. Scientific books too were commonly written in Latin so that they could be read in all countries with equal ease.

Thus it was natural for the good Pastor Linnaeus to teach his son, from the age of four, to name all the flowers in the gardens and meadows by their Latin titles. And it was simple enough for little Carl to learn that this stately tree was *Populus* (poplar) and that prickly bush was a *Juniperus* (juniper). Nor will it take you long to guess what Pastor Linnaeus meant by *Rosa, Lilium, Viola, Orchis, Geranium, Pinus, Hyacinthus,* or *Tulipa.* Latin is a melodious language and so like our own that it is easy to understand hundreds of words in it at first sight.

Not that it was easy for the pastor's son to become a scientist. He was so poor that just to live was a struggle, and learning was another since in those days the few books there were about natural history were not only expensive and difficult but were most of them based on the work of the great Greek scientists of two thousand years earlier. Wise as those men were, for their times, the Greeks in their Golden Age knew nothing about northern Europe. Thus often a student in Germany or Sweden, finding a plant that wasn't in one of these old books, just threw the specimen away as a clumsy mistake and gave Nature a low grade. The book couldn't be wrong!

CARL LINNAEUS

That is why a professor at the Swedish university at Upsala was surprised one April day in 1729 to discover a student in the botanical garden who was not looking up the flowers in a book but, on the contrary, appeared to be writing a book about what he observed for himself. This originality so broke all the rules of the day, that the professor spoke to the lad. He noted how poor the boy must be; he was thin and pale from undernourishment, and there was paper

stuffing his worn shoe soles. But his mind was ablaze with ideas. So impressed with young Carl Linnaeus was this professor that he took him to call on Dr. Rudbeck, the only man on the faculty with a wide knowledge of natural history. And kindly old Rudbeck was so delighted with Carl that he gave him a room and meals in his own house and made the boy free of his library.

In return, Linnaeus finally presented his host with the manuscript of a little book he had written. It explained the fact (then known to few people and only dimly understood) that flowers have sex, just as animals have. They are male and female, Linnaeus showed, and in their own way (by pollination) they mate. They bring forth young of their own kind when the ripe fruit swells and the seeds are released.

By the way, if you have any trouble in remembering which parts of the flower are male and produce pollen, then listen for the sound of *men* in "sta*men*," and you'll never forget that stamens are male. I can't think of anything specially female about the word "pistil." But I've heard it claimed that girls stand still, when told to, just a little better than the restless boys. The pi*stils* stand in the center of most flowers, and the stamens usually stand in a ring outside them, just inside the petals.

Linnaeus intently examined all the flowers he could, and soon discovered that by counting the number of stamens and of pistils in each, every kind of flower could be fitted into a neat system of classification. Here is just a fragment of that system to show you how it works:

1 stamen—	1 pistil:	*Canna*
2 stamens—	1 pistil:	*Lilac*
3 stamens—	1 pistil:	*Iris*
	2 pistils:	*Grasses*
	3 pistils:	*Jagged Chickweed*
5 stamens—	1 pistil:	*Violet*
	2 pistils:	*Gentian*
	5 pistils:	*Flax*
10 stamens—	1 pistil:	*Indian-Pipes*
	2 pistils:	*Carnation*
	5 pistils:	*Common Chickweed*

And so on up to: many stamens, many pistils: *Water Lily*

Linnaeus also took account of the number and position and shape of the petals. The irregular form of the orchids with their curious hanging lips sets them off in a family of their own. The composite (compound) heads of sunflowers and their kin, the daisies, thistles, asters, and dandelions, put them all in the great family called the composites, a family as important in the temperate zone as are orchids in the tropics.

Having made a start on this system of classification based on form, Linnaeus wished to test it on the flora of some other place. So with the encouragement of his friend Rudbeck, he set out for Lapland, the far-northern part of Sweden where the Lapps and the reindeer live, the land of the midnight sun and the brief but enchanting arctic wild flowers. He rode out on horseback one May morning from the gates of the old university. The grass was springing, the larks were singing, fresh air filled his lungs, and excite-

ment tingled in his young veins. While other students left Upsala
to go on to book learning at the universities of Heidelberg, Oxford, Leyden, and Padua, Linnaeus turned to the field, as scientists
say. His was the first natural history expedition. Only one man
went on it, but this was the one right man. His equipment was
little more than a magnifying glass, a yardstick, a notebook, and
an inkwell. But a genius was going to look through that little lens
and write in that immortal notebook.

When he returned, Linnaeus had followed the birds to their arctic nesting grounds and had explored and named the wide-eyed arctic wild flowers. And his system for classifying them worked perfectly.

It worked so well when applied by the Dutch to all the strange flora that their sailors brought home, that the West India Company offered Linnaeus a well-paid position to come and serve them. The King of Spain sent him an invitation to become court botanist. An Oxford professor offered to share his salary with him if he would teach there. He preferred, after one trip to Holland, France, and England, to remain in Upsala as a professor. To him flocked students from every country, and presently students trained by Linnaeus went forth to every part of the globe. To the deserts of Arabia, the South African veldt, the virgin forests of North America; to Ceylon, and the then unknown continent of Australia. Some died of fever or exhaustion, martyrs to science. All sent back specimens to the wise, kindly old Swedish professor.

The names Linnaeus gave the animals and plants were Latin of course. He didn't invent this custom; what he did was to pare down the long, wordy Latin descriptions used for names in those times to just two. In the same way you have two names, just as Linnaeus had two: Linnaeus, to show that he was a member of the Linnaeus family, and Carl, to set him forth distinctly from all others in it. Thus Linnaeus named the dog rose *Rosa canina*, and the eglantine rose *Rosa eglanteria*. (He named our common black-eyed susan *Rudbeckia hirta*, after his old benefactor Rudbeck.) He named the lion *Felis leo*, the tiger *Felis tigris*, the common tabby *Felis cattus*. So all three members of the feline tribe (naturalists say "genus") of Felis are indicated as related to each other. Anyone looking at a cat, lion, and tiger, can feel this relationship, but it takes Linnaeus's two-name system to express it neatly and clearly.

For of course the animal kingdom, just like the plant kingdom, can be set in order by a close study of its forms. It is easier to take a daisy apart and count its petals than it is to take apart a lion, but the principle of classification into a two-name species works as well. Cats, tigers, and lions are classified together because (among other reasons) they have pretty much the same kind and number of teeth—suited to their lives as meat-eaters. All mammals are now classified in part by their teeth, including the human species.

Make a count of your teeth and you'll see that you have two pairs, in each jaw, of incisor teeth—your front teeth, used for cutting and tearing. On each side of these there is a long sharp cuspid or "dog" tooth. Then come the premolar teeth for light grinding, and at the back of the mouth are the heavy molars for a thorough chewing.

So we could write out the formula for human teeth this way:

	INCISORS	CUSPIDS	PREMOLARS	MOLARS			
Upper	2–2	1–1	2–2	3–3	(counting wisdom teeth)		
Lower	2–2	1–1	2–2	3–3	"	"	"

Now look at the formula for that chisel-toothed bark-chewer, the beaver:

	INCISORS	CUSPIDS	PREMOLARS	MOLARS
Upper	1–1	0–0	1–1	3–3
Lower	1–1	0–0	1–1	3–3

You can see that beavers have no use for cuspids, since they don't tear up meat. Try to guess what sort of an animal has this formula:

	INCISORS	CUSPIDS	PREMOLARS	MOLARS
Upper	3–3	1–1	4–4	2–2
Lower	3–3	1–1	4–4	3–3

Here's a hint: "What long teeth you have, Grandmother!" said Little Red Ridinghood.

Here's a common animal with no dog teeth and more incisors and premolars in the upper jaw than in the lower jaw. What would you say about its eating habits?

	INCISORS	CUSPIDS	PREMOLARS	MOLARS
Upper	2–2	0–0	3–3	3–3
Lower	1–1	0–0	2–2	3–3

Yes, it's Br'er Rabbit, the buck-toothed cottontail, who nibbles lettuce and carrot tops right out of our garden and eats your mother's pansies and delphiniums.

Now hold a piece of fish over your cat's head till she howls for it with wide-open mouth. Then write out her dental formula. If you do this correctly you're already a naturalist. But if you compare her teeth with a lion's by putting your head in the lion's

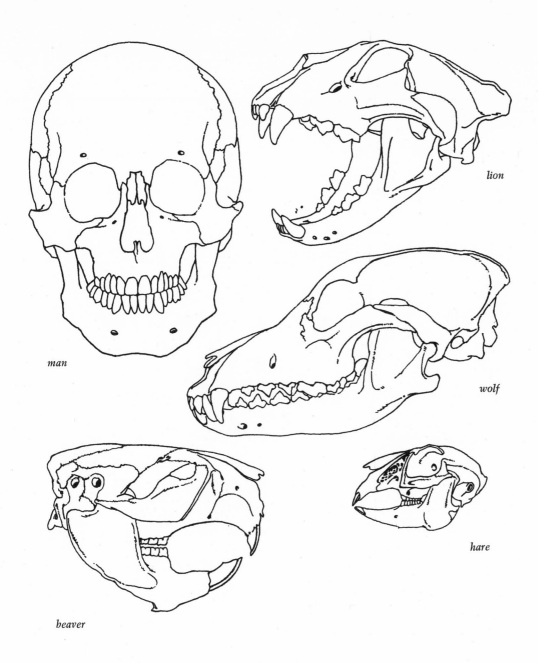

lion

man

wolf

beaver

hare

mouth, you'll be one more martyr to science. I guess Linnaeus counted a dead lion's teeth. Anyway he lived to a ripe old age—after having proved to all the world that animals and plants must be classified by their form and structure.

V.

HOURS
AND
SEASONS

SLEEP AND SNOW

WHEN winter is upon us, when the leaves are all fallen and dead, when the nights are long and biting and the days, at best, but short, Nature seems to have slammed a door shut in our faces. The beauty of color is gone; not a lonely cricket skirls his song from the frozen grass, not a frog trills from the pond locked in the grip of ice. And under your heels, hard as a cold heart, rings the frostbitten earth. There is no bird song but the screech of the little owl in the night, and the hoarse *Who-the-deuce-are-you?* of the great horned owl, silent-winged pirate of the winter nights.

Presently come high winds and blizzards, sleet storms and zero weather. Planes are grounded; trains and cars are stalled; sometimes schools are dismissed early when a bad storm is known to be coming. At such times we are too busy looking after ourselves to think what is happening to the animals. Sleet in particular paralyzes bird life; when a bird's wings are ice-laden it cannot fly and so cannot forage for food. I have seen a tree sparrow fall dead of starvation and cold off a bare bough. When blizzard winds blow with gale force, I have found as many as fifty little juncos under the eaves fluffing their feathers, shuffling their feet, softly chittering—talking about the weather, I suppose, just like us. In very bitter weather I have seen the horned larks, Lapland longspurs, wintering chickadees, bobwhites, and snow buntings dive right into a snowbank—to get warm! For of course snow, being frozen water vapor, is the temperature at which water freezes everywhere —32 degrees above zero. When it is crusted over on top, even when the air is 20 degrees below zero, the air in the snow helps to make it a cozy cover.

After the days begin to grow longer, but still long before spring, you realize that there is a lot more winter bird life than most people suspect. Sunflower seeds and suet and crumbs will soon bring the birds right to your window—woodpeckers and goldfinches, cedar waxwings, song sparrows and the gorgeous red cardinal and his pretty wife, white-breasted nuthatches, tufted titmice, the jolly chickadees and juncos (known by their white "shirttails" seen sticking out of their tail feathers as they fly away), and the tuneful tree sparrows who sometimes warble all together, on sunny winter days, in a sort of singing society.

The white-throated sparrows utter their "quarrier note"—a little metallic *clink* like a hammer dropping on stones in a quarry. Sometimes the tiny golden-crowned kinglets utter a faltering fife-like warble that rises and then seems to fall in an explosive cascade of notes. Even the city starlings splutter out something between a wolf whistle and a curse. It sounds to me like SWEET . . . *Beelzebub!* And if you are lucky you may hear the meadowlarks whistling wistfully from the frozen weed tops, or flush a covey of horned larks that rise with a sharp plaintive cry, wheel around, and then settle back in the same place.

Of course no cold-blooded creature can stay abroad in winter. When it's below freezing, their blood temperature falls too low to allow them to stir. So the lizards and frogs, toads, salamanders, and snakes must all creep away to some hiding place and doze the winter away. They begin to find a napping place long before the weather immobilizes them. Rattlesnakes collect from miles around into dens in the rocks—where nobody cares to disturb them! Toads and frogs burrow deep in the mud. And some of the warm-blooded mammals, too, decide to sleep the whole season away. Bats travel hundreds of miles, if need be, to certain caves known to them for

generations, and there, hanging upside down, they slumber all winter in big dormitories. Woodchucks, fairly waddling with their autumn coat of fat, toddle away to bed below ground. Chipmunks and ground squirrels do the same, and the red squirrel of the north woods holes up in a hollow tree to doze.

This deep unconsciousness of certain animals in winter is nothing like the ordinary nighttime sleep. It is called hibernation, and a hibernating frog is so deep down in this strange slumber that he becomes insensitive to any pain, though a frog that is merely sleeping will awaken to the slightest pinprick. You might think you could compare hibernation to the condition of a human who is under an anesthetic. But that would be a mistake. Anesthetized people breathe faster than normal, and their heartbeats quicken. Just the opposite with the hibernator; his heartbeats grow so slow and faint they can hardly be detected; he may breathe only once in many minutes, and that only faintly. His temperature drops till he seems cold as stone. So he remains, nourished by his fat the winter long, to awaken only when spring returns.

Hibernation, of course, doesn't take place in regions with very mild winters. Nor do many mammals hibernate in the arctic either, for the ground, just a few inches under the surface, is frozen so hard the year around that creatures cannot burrow into it. Hibernation is, then, a habit that goes with the cool-temperate part of the Northern Hemisphere. If you mapped on the globe the parts of the world where it is a frequent thing, hibernation would lie in about the same zone as the winter-naked or drop-leaf trees. Indeed, in their own way, maples and beeches, birches and aspens, might be said to hibernate too.

Arctic mammals and birds either have to migrate to warmer regions in winter or stay active right through the season of the long snows. Many wear snowy coats, like the polar bear and the arctic fox. It must be difficult for their prey to see these hunters coming through the snow. But the hunted too may be camouflaged by white coats. Ptarmigans in winter are largely white in plumage. And that big-footed hare called the snowshoe rabbit varies from a brown summer coat to a suit of winter white. Some of the blood-

thirsty little weasels change from a dark summer fur to a costume all white in winter except for the black hairs on the tips of their tails. Their pelts are then called ermine, and so beautiful is ermine fur—pure white with black tips—and so expensive (because it takes many pelts to make a cloak or coat), that only great rulers, nobles in coronation robes, and ladies of wealth can afford ermine. Yet there may be plenty of live ermine trotting around on all fours right in your neighborhood, for weasels both in winter and summer linger around every chicken yard. The trouble is that you can look right at a weasel in winter white and not see it against the snow. But here is the print of his tracks:

In winter the animals who don't hibernate seem more active than in summer. They have to be, to keep alive! Most of them are too stealthy to come out much in the day, but their night-prowling can't be concealed once the snow comes. If you will look outside your door after a fresh snowfall, you'll be astounded at the maze of footprints left by animal visitors. The fun comes in untangling them, for each species leaves its own characteristic print.

Let's start with your dog, since you can see him making tracks and so check up on the truthfulness of this picture. Here is his familiar, firm, full print:

You can see just where your cat went last night by following her tracks as she stepped gingerly through the snow, probably stopping to shake each paw if the stuff was too wet:

And now for her enemy the common house rat. Notice that this wicked pest does not stroll or prowl; it moves—unless fleeing for its life—by jumps, as you can see:

The following imprints look as though they had been made by a baby, but a baby with very small crooked feet. This is one baby not to follow up too closely—or you'll arrive at the business end of a skunk!

Of all snow prints the quaintest is that of the cottontail rabbit, who is also a jumper. You will see that his footmarks are almost a comic cartoon of a rabbit's face, with those big pricked-up ears, little wobbly nose, and mouth like a little round O!

But there is a joker in this joke. For when the rabbit jumps he lands with his hind feet foremost! They make the ears of the snow cartoon; the nose and mouth are made by the front feet which land behind! If you didn't know this, you might be inclined to track a rabbit by his footfall—backward. I have heard of a boy who did, and this was his report: "I followed him right to the place where he was sitting—and he wasn't there!"

When in no hurry, the short-tailed field mouse leaves clues like this:

But when he's scared, he makes tracks in this wise:

His long-tailed cousin the white-footed mouse drags that tail, and you can see its wobbly line running through his footprints:

If tracks begin and end at a tree, you can be sure it's a squirrel who made them. Thus, to see what they look like, just do a little sleuthing on your own in the nearest city park, suburban street, or country grove. So here I'll end, leaving you a blank space to draw your own squirrel tracks after you've discovered them:

SPRING FEVER

ONE March morning, after you've waited for spring until you thought it would never come, there is a tenderness at last in the blue of the sky; there's a swift unchaining of the ice-locked brooks that now come seething over their banks. There's a smell of leaf smoke coming up on the south wind; people are burning last year's dead foliage, laying bare the pale green of their lawns and the first slender shoots of crocus. In the still-leafless thickets the alders hang out their slim catkins, and song sparrows, as if they had been long corked up, are suddenly un-stopped and bubble over in melody.

So does spring come stealing up to us from the South, where redbud is flowering on the old red hills of Georgia, and mockingbirds are whistling in the street palms in Carolina. It blows in on

192

the soft air through the open window and touches your cheek as you sit at your desk trying to keep your mind on your lessons. You can smell the warming earth in it; you even think you catch the scent of faraway first things blooming secretly in the woods. You don't hear what the teacher is saying; you have lost your place in the book; you jump when you are called on. In fact, you have spring fever.

And you are not the only one. The wild flowers themselves have, literally, a spring fever of their own.

Inside the pulpit of the little jack-in-the-pulpit, it's definitely warm. When the air is 62 degrees chilly, a young dandelion may run a temperature of 130 degrees. And one of the frailest little flowers in the world, the exquisite snowdrop, grown here in gardens but a wild flower in Switzerland, is actually able to melt the snow around and above it. Indeed, many flowers of the Swiss Alps can thus bloom beneath a hard crust of ice, snugly encased in a hollow sphere of crystal.

The explanation lies in the heat of rapid growth. Swift growing in plants uses up a great deal of oxygen, just as running makes you breathe fast. When you run and breathe hard, with oxygen being used up in your body, you soon grow warm even on a cold day. So it is with the growing flower or swelling bud; the temperature of rapid plant-breathing may be enough to melt snow and ice.

If you keep a day-to-day record of bloomings in your neighborhood, you'll find out that the first plants to flower are not the pretty, tremulous anemones, or that sunny tramp the dandelion, nor yet the fair hepaticas, but the pines, cedars, spruce trees, larches, willows, poplars, alders, and hazels—all trees with the kind of flower called a catkin. These fuzzy or silky spikes of bloom, soft as a kitten's tail, don't look like flowers in the least since they have no petals. Indeed, the male spikes consist in little more than anthers or pollen sacs. The female ones are mostly ovaries containing unfertilized "eggs" awaiting the pollen.

Now these very ancient types of flowers, without perfume or petals, came early into the world. When they first appeared in geologic history, bees and other flower-loving insects had not come into being. These old types of trees just loosed their buoyant pollen in great storms of golden waste upon the bee-less, butterfly-less winds. And still today these first trees to bloom fling out their pollen in a drifting cloud before a single bee or butterfly is stirring. About the time that the first flowers with petals and perfume evolved on that long-ago earth, the first flower-loving insects became common. As if the springtime were telling over again in brief form this story of evolution, the insect-pollinated flowers spread their sweet petals at just the season when the honeybees come out, followed in turn by bumblebees, butterflies, and hummingbirds.

Now the Mayflower or trailing arbutus breathes its exquisite odor in the woods; now the bird's-foot violet appears on the hills, its two upper petals a rich pansy purple, the three lower ones a radiant blue-lavender. The solitary bloodroot leaf unfurls, like a blue-green banner of some tiny supernatural nation, beside the frail white flower. And near it in the woods, Dutchman's-breeches dance quaintly beside the bluets called also innocence and Quaker-ladies for their prim sweetness. Spring-beauties spread a pink carpet underneath the little wild plum trees whose white blossoms foam upon the bare twigs. And then the great white trillium shines like a three-pointed star down the aisles of the trees, and the deep red trillium gives out its odor of crushed strawberries. They call it, from the date of its blooming, the whippoorwill-flower, just as the fair white shadblow is named for that week in spring when shad swim up from the Atlantic to breed in our rivers.

Most of our early spring flowers bloom in the woods, but while the trees are still bare or just leafing out. They are making the most of the sunlight before it is cut off by summer's dense shade. The dark forest earth absorbs the warmth of sunlight better than any other kind of soil just as your dark clothes are warmer than light-colored ones. By the time the leaves overhead are out, the spring flowers are faded. For a little while, thereafter, the leaves of blood-root, violets, wild ginger, and Dutchman's-breeches grow large and thick; then they too wither away, and you forget their dainty charm in the splendor of summer flowers. Even if you remember them, you can't even find where they were—so completely have they vanished. But they live on, under the soil, in their little bulbs or small tubers or compact, root-like underground stems.

If it's hard enough to keep your mind on your studies when the warm breeze dances into the schoolroom bearing tales of flowers in bloom, it's worse when right outside the window the birds call you to come out. The robin probably got you up first in the morning with his *Cheer up, cheery! Wake up, weary!* The song sparrow

has a tune to which some people put the words: *Maids, maids, maids, put on your tea kettle-ettle-ettle-ettle!* On the shore and the wet meadow, the killdeer plover tells his own name plaintively, *Killdee! Killdee!* as he flies off as though he were wounded. The

mourning dove doesn't really mourn but sounds serenely contented, repeating over and over his *AH! Coo . . . coo . . . cooo!* The
flicker on the oak trunks rattles his watchman's rattle—*Flickup,*
wickup, wickup! The meadowlark on a fence post tosses into the
sun his sweet windy whistle of *Et-seedy-yew! Et-SEELY-ew!* and

the chickadee fools you by giving, instead of his own name, an im-
itation of the phoebe, a thin *FEE-bee!* And the grackles with their
gabbling, whistling, creaking chatter, forever streaking off in flocks
only to come spattering back to the same tree, just about complete
the list of early songsters.

April has almost twice as many new bird songs to learn as March
offered, and May three times as many as April. The chewink says
his name, and the chipping sparrow chips, and the house wren has
well been called "a barrelful of song in a pint of bird." The red-
eyed vireo has a conversational little refrain, like a human slowly
asking little questions: "Where ya goin'? . . . Whatcha doin'? . . .
D'ya hear me? . . . Can you see me? *Now* you see me. . . . No, you
don't. . . ." He's a dull-colored little bird who keeps to the tree tops,
so that it may be long before you see him, but you can know him
by the sound of his teasing.

Not any music box or piano, violin, or even flute ever sounds like a bird, even when the bird song is written in notes and played on the instrument. For birds don't stick to our musical scale; they sing quarter tones and eighth tones when they want to; they hang onto a trill like a prima donna, or throw in so many rapid grace notes that the ear cannot remember or record them. And in that pulsing feathered throat there is a special song box called a syrinx. We humans have one called a larynx, but it is not the same; only the birds have this particular organ of voice that can give forth either the harsh caw of the raven or the wild laughing bells of the canyon wren, the serene utterance of the evening thrush or the bluejay's raucous boast as he sails from tree to tree.

What rapture to be able to pour forth song like a nightingale's or a mockingbird's! What delight to be able to sing out all the joy of a morning in spring, to tell the world in airy, original music! But the truth of it is that birds don't sing just for happiness. Bird song is mostly a male affair, and it is uttered chiefly to proclaim territory as belonging especially to the singer. Rather as your dog declares by his barks that this is his home ground, the male bird sings out to all others that this particular neighborhood is the one he considers his own, where he means to mate and nest as master. So any other male of his kind enters the song-posted territory of the singer only at his own peril. And any female just arriving from the south understands that the singer is offering her the protection of his territorial rights. If she accepts them she becomes his mate. What with all the singing and blooming and mating going on, the whole world, by May, seems to have caught spring fever!

JOURNEYS AND RETURNS

ALL of us delight in the "trusty almanac of the birds' first coming back," as Emerson called it. From every dooryard tree, from marsh and shore and meadow, come the springtime cries and songs of the returning birds. The first to appear—robins, bluebirds, redwing blackbirds, song sparrows, and chickadees—have come but a short distance, from no farther than the southern states or even perhaps the southern part of your own state. Then, about a month later, the black and orange oriole (named, for no good reason, the Baltimore), and the scarlet tanager, and many another from the tropics begin to pour in. Last of all to arrive are some of the shore birds like the plovers, curlews, and yellowlegs, for they have come the greatest distance—from the prairies or pampas of Argentina, south of the equator, where

199

it is summer while we are having winter. These birds are usually on their way to nest in the Far North, on the arctic prairies called tundras. So they are strictly migrants, not summer residents as are the orioles and tanagers.

Migrants and summer residents together may be so numerous on a day in late spring that a sharp-eyed "birder" can chalk up as many as one hundred different species seen in a single day. Of a fine warm morning then, especially between five and six o'clock, you can see more birds right at your door than at any other time of year. For such a day and such an hour mark the high point of the spring migration.

Not only birds but many kinds of animals migrate. Some fishes, like the salmon, follow a regular route, breeding in the same spot in the same river, then going back to the same locality in the ocean, year after year. Seagoing mammals commonly migrate, especially seals, sea lions, walruses, and sea otters, whose breeding grounds are in the Far North. Some bats migrate on their leathery wings, although others hibernate in caves.

What is this seasonal journey called a migration? It is not just a search for food, nor is it an exodus or "drive" away from an area of overpopulation such as is made sometimes by great hordes of lemming mice that hurry into the sea and drown themselves or by swarms of grasshoppers that eat up everything in their path like a plague. Nor is it an invasion of new territory as rats from Europe, escaping from ships, have invaded some of the Pacific

islands or as rabbits have invaded Australia, brought there by mistaken mankind. Migration is a very special kind of animal travel. If I weren't afraid of being laughed at by my fellow naturalists, I would say that migration is a two-way ticket on a honeymoon. With all the new clothes, new surroundings, and new feelings that go with honeymoons.

Let's follow the caribou, an animal that enjoys its honeymoon in autumn rather than spring. This member of the deer family (distinguished by the fact that the females wear antlers too) is found all around the north polar regions; it is, in fact, almost the same as the common or Santa Claus reindeer. In Lapland, where it is domesticated for its milk, meat, and hide, and also used as a beast of burden, it is often kept in pens and gets no chance to migrate. In North America, where it is free to roam, it is called by the Micmac Indian name of caribou, and its mass migrations are a tremendous event. A single herd may take days to pass a given spot; their hooves cut the wild sod to ribbons, and the earth shakes with their tramplings, the air with their grunting and bellowing.

Now when the caribou come north in spring, they aren't a very beautiful sight. Their heavy winter coats are shedding in ugly patches, leaving them looking moth-eaten. The females, great with young, lumber clumsily along, stopping to give birth to the fawns wherever the event overtakes them. But after an invigorating summer in the Far North, caribou are ready for the autumn mating season. The mighty antlers are full grown and rubbed clean of woolly hairs. The male wears a magnificent throat ruff of shining white, and the female a similar one, but not so heavy, of demure gray. Then when the mating season is over, the antlers are shed, as surely as the leaves drop from the balsam poplars overhead. The males gradually draw off into all-male herds, the females into their own groups, and the yearlings into adolescent "clubs."

What you notice about the caribous' annual life cycle is that they not only make a great mass movement—the whole race deserting one region and moving steadily toward another—but their lives are completely changed. In different seasons they behave differently, they certainly look different, and we can be sure they have very different feelings.

It is the same with the migratory birds. As they fly northward to us now in spring, the males are in their bright new bridal dress; their throats are full of song; their thoughts, or at least their feel-

ings, are all of mating, and they are ready to fight a rival at any moment. But when the courting season finally ends, the males gradually lose their voices until in the hottest part of the year they are often completely without song. They begin to moult too; some ducks lose so many wing feathers at once that they cannot fly for a time and have to drift helplessly, unable to rise from the water. And even when the change to a winter plumage is complete, male birds are much less colorful; they may closely resemble the females

in dress or even their own sons. In fall they show no interest in their former mates, and males, females, and young all take their separate departures for the south.

So different may be the appearance and feeding habits of migratory birds that some of them receive different names in their winter and summer homes. The beautiful little redstart of our northern states moults his fine bridal plumage before he reaches the West Indies in December. His arrival in that month causes him to be called the Christmas bird. Our merry, tuneful male bobolink, with his beautiful black, white, and yellow bridal costume, is in fall an uninteresting-looking bird, in plumage hardly distinguishable from the female. And he shifts from a summer

diet of insects to a diet in our southern states of the wild and cultivated kinds of rice. There he is naturally called the rice bird, and he eats himself thoroughly fat and grows as sluggish (for a bird) as he is voiceless of any jingling tune. Such changes in name hint that the birds make as great a change in a single season as humans do in twenty years—a change like that from, let us say, little-girlhood to motherhood. The difference is that birds, having each spring grown up enough to mate and have children, "grow down" again each winter, completely forgetting all their bridal joys and parental cares! Only to remember or at least experience them all again at the same time next spring.

And birds are wondrously prompt, steady, and faithful about their returns. The Canada goose moves northward no faster than spring itself, taking care to stay just south of the melting point of the ice on the lakes and rivers, so that he has open water in which to alight. Chimney swifts, which can shoot forward more than 150 miles an hour in a burst of speed, take only nine days to go nine hundred miles on migration. That is far faster than most

birds make it. Most of our songbirds do not travel at great heights either; usually migrating by night, they prefer to stay about 50 to 250 feet above the surface of the earth. Only day-fliers, like the cranes and herons and other birds with mighty wings, sometimes soar up to about ten thousand feet altitude, cruising along at a steady clip and eyeing the landmarks below them.

For birds know their way around the world just as thoroughly as our pilots. Take the arctic tern, for instance. Some of these long-winged, graceful, gull-like sea birds nest as far north as the northern tip of Ellesmere Island. Get out your map and you'll see that that is only five hundred miles from the North Pole. Yet the baby tern hatched there this summer will, in six months, be twelve thousand miles away, fishing in the waters off the frozen continent of Antarctica. He may have gone by way of Iceland, visited the coast of the British Isles and Spain, the western shore of Africa, then the coasts of Brazil, and finally the Antarctic Circle. On the way back he may skirt the Cape of Good Hope and the coast of tropical Africa before heading for North America and Ellesmere

Island again. The total round trip will be about twenty-four thousand miles, in a grand figure 8, and the tern will have crossed the equator twice and the Atlantic ocean four times!

Just as astounding is the skill birds sometimes show in finding their way back to the very spot where they nested last year. Phoebes commonly return to the undersides of the same bridge—out of all the bridges in their summer home range. Wrens often return to the same wren box, and purple martins to the same martin house put up for them by their human friends. Chimney swifts, out of a city wilderness of chimneys, remember a particular one; the same swifts probably return to your chimney year after year.

We know it is the same bird (or pair of birds) that returns to the identical nesting site because all over this country, and in many other lands, there are people who make an enthusiastic, scientific, and useful hobby of bird banding. To band a bird, the bander baits a harmless little box trap with birdseed and suet. Many times a day the bander visits the trap; he lifts out any bird guest that has dropped in for a free lunch, and then the bander fixes around one bird leg a tiny aluminum ring. On this is stamped a serial number like the number on an auto license. And just as every auto license plate is registered in your state capital with the name and address of the owner and the date when the license was taken out, so in the national capital of Washington and in Canada's capital at Ottawa all these bird numbers are kept on record by the two governments.

Birds once trapped soon learn to come to other traps for food and a little petting, and so on their great travels they may show up at one banding station after another. Each time they do so, the banders turn in the information to their government's central bureau. And even if the bird is found dead, the finder, it is hoped, will send in the tag. In this way scientists literally keep tabs on

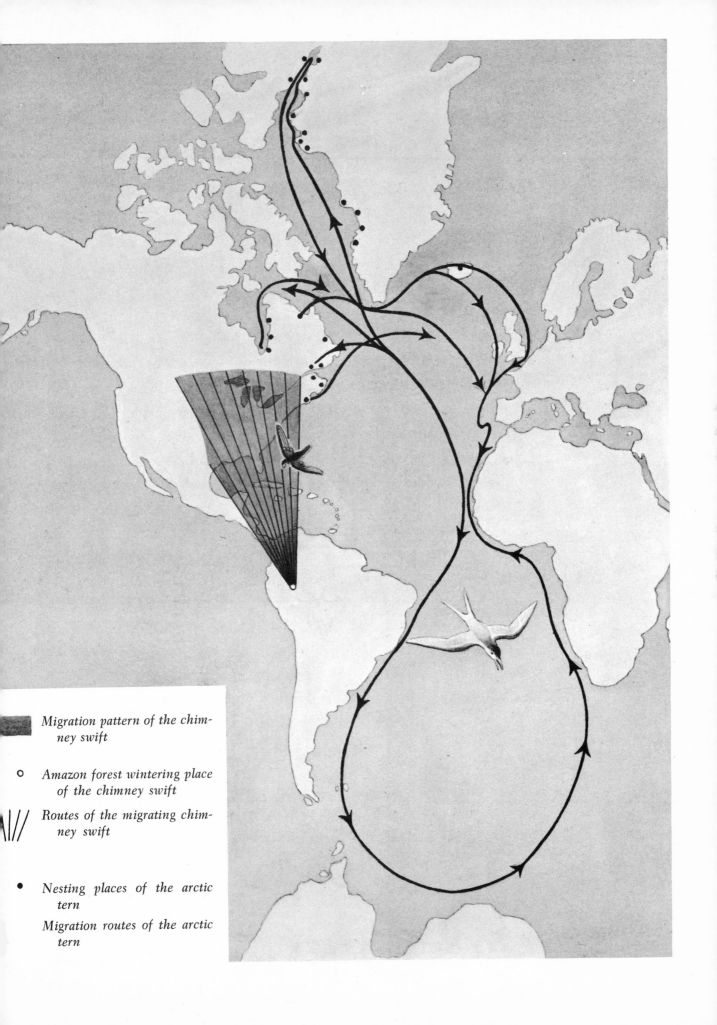

Migration pattern of the chimney swift

○   Amazon forest wintering place
of the chimney swift

\|//   Routes of the migrating chim-
ney swift

●   Nesting places of the arctic
tern

Migration routes of the arctic
tern

the birds in their travels. In many cases we know where a certain bird has been from babyhood, for banders frequently band chicks in the nest. Thus we can discover whether young birds fly before, with, or after the older ones. We know exactly where hundreds of kinds of birds spend their winters, and where they go to nest in summer.

But for a long time it seemed that even banding would not reveal the secret of the chimney swifts' migration. Though more than thirty thousand bands were attached to swifts' legs, in the eastern United States and Canada, and though these sooty little travelers entered traps in great number in our southern states, nobody knew what on earth became of them in winter. Then in May of 1941 an American engineer, deep in the remotest parts of the Amazon forest, saw an Indian chief wearing a necklace made out of thirteen aluminum bird bands—taken from the legs of swifts he had shot. The engineer got the bands from the chief by barter and sent them to the American consul in Lima, Peru. Then they were forwarded to the State Department in Washington, which turned them over to the Fish and Wildlife Service. And there the serial numbers were looked up, and these proved that the feathered wearers had come mainly from Tennessee, but some from Illinois, and one from Kingston, Ontario. However wide apart their nesting places, all swifts, it now appears, spend their winters in a very small area in one of the least explored parts of the tropics— "east of the Andes and west of nowhere."

THE CLOAK OF NIGHT

As twilight deepens into night, there come to your ears last little snatches of song and sleepy cries of contentment as the songbirds make ready for shut-eye. But owls are opening their staring, amber eyes, which have blinked sulkily all day; the first sweet quavering trill of the screech owl comes from the trees, while the great horned owl gives his barking hoots. The day-time hawks go wheeling away down the sky to their nightly perches, screaming no more their war cry of *killy, killy, killy!* Instead, the nighthawks (no relation to the day hawks, but rather to the whippoorwill) follow each other in a dark formation across the sky.

Red squirrels are snuggling down together in their hollow trees just as their deadly foe, the prowling marten, begins to creep along the pine branches. Bees have all left the flowers and are safe in their hive by now, but the midges, newly hatched, are doing a mad wedding dance above the surface of the lake and the tops of the bordering trees. The diurnal (day-active) butterflies have gone to rest beneath the leaves; their relatives the moths, which are mostly nocturnal (night-active), are just emerging, the males' feathery antennae all a-quiver for the enticing perfume of the nocturnal flowers and for any sweet-scented female of their kind.

Thus every species that goes to sleep at the approach of dark seems matched by another that is just awakening. Night, for half of the animal world, is the best part of each twenty-four hours. We humans find this hard to imagine, for Nature made us diurnal animals. Our eyesight is good enough by day, but poor by night.

Our blunted sense of smell gives us little knowledge of what moves
and lives all around us, though scent carries best in the dews and
damps of night. And our range of hearing is so short at both the
upper and lower ends of the scale that we don't know the half of
what's being whispered, squeaked, boomed, grunted, promised,
begged for, or murmured in what seems to us the silent night. So
that there is nothing much a human can do out-of-doors in the
dark but bump into things, fall off edges, step unawares into
water, and generally scare himself. I've found, when camping in
the woods without light, that there is just nothing to do but go to
sleep like the birds on the bough and the squirrels in the hollow
trunk.

But while we sleep our fellow mammals come out, sniff about,
prowl, catch a meal, explore for mates. Raccoons, skunks, foxes,

bears, coyotes, deer, bobcats, wild mice and rats, shrews, weasels, minks, and moose are all mainly nocturnal. True, you may see any or all of these abroad by day—sometimes. But whether hunters

or hunted, they are happiest under the cloak of night. Some that have little to fear from any other wild creatures don't hesitate to make a lot of night noise. A moose will come crashing through the woods, bathe lustily in the lily ponds, pull his clumsy feet out of the muck he loves, and blat uproariously, like a late party-goer who forgets that others are in bed.

If you want to test how much night life there is all around you, just go out with a flashlight after dark. The first thing you may see, if you shine the light on the grass, will be night crawlers. These are fat earthworms. They have no eyes to see your flash, but they are ultra-sensitive to vibrations. They feel (rather than hear) your footsteps, and, lying with their tails in their burrows, they

pop back before you come. But if you will wear sneakers and glide your feet along without lifting them, you can come right up to the night crawlers and capture them with your hands. They make fine fishing bait.

And your flashlight will pick up the reflected gleam in the eyes of many animals. To get the most out of this kind of exploring, hold the light alongside your temple on a level with your own eyes; if you carry the flash at hip-height, the angle of the light from the creature's eyes may not be such that you can see the reflection. For reflection it is. The animals have a mirror-like layer over the retina of their eyes, called the tapetum, which throws back the light of your flash, and of auto headlights and house lights.

And each kind of creature reflects from its eyes particular colors; thus your dog's kind brown or black eyes appear at night to roll with an opal fire. Your cat's eyes are apt to be an eerie green. Siamese cats, when angry or frightened, have fiery eyes when shined on. Bears at night reflect an angry red from their small, surly eyes. Frogs and toads give off pink, pale yellow and white reflections, and spiders' eyes shine very softly with an unearthly green or pale blue light or an intense silver like a drop of quicksilver. Deer reflect orange from their eyes and are so fascinated by the light of lamps that hunters used to "shine for deer"—that is, attract them by torchlight and then shoot them while they stood still, unable to see the man and gun behind the torch. This is now, quite rightly, illegal. But auto headlights will often make deer stop on the road, and if your car stops too, you can get a long look at these beautiful nocturnal creatures. When you want to go ahead, blow your horn or slam the car door, and the deer will bound out of the way unhurt.

The eyes of nocturnal animals are especially fitted to help them see in the dark, partly because the center or pupil of the eye can be widened by the delicate muscles that control the iris, or colored part. Your eyes can do the same but to a lesser extent. When you enter a motion-picture theater from a bright street, at first you are

unable to see which seats are empty because your pupils are still narrowed against the brilliance of the outside lights. Gradually, without your having to think about it, the muscles of your irises pull your pupils more widely open, admitting more light, and then you find a seat quite easily. So with the eyes of nocturnal animals, but their pupils can open far wider than ours, as you know from looking in an owl's great staring orbs. Probably nights that look pitch-dark to us are about as well illuminated for cats, dogs, foxes, and owls as full moonlight makes the scenery appear to our eyes.

And what an owl can't see, it can hear with those great sensitive, movable ears. Almost all nocturnal creatures have a sense of hearing far more acute than ours. Bats, indeed, use their enormous ears to judge the distances of things in the dark. Constantly they give out high-pitched squeaks above the range of human hearing. They judge, by the time it takes an echo to bounce back to them, just how near an object is in the dark. In this way it has been found by careful experiment that bats, flying at top speed around an absolutely lightless room that has been strung with fine wires

going every whichway, can avoid striking a single wire. The principle of timing the echo is now used on ships to tell how deep is the water beneath the ship. By echoes it is possible to map the whole ocean bottom, avoid running on rocks, icebergs, and shoals, and even detect submarines. But we didn't think this up ourselves; we applied the principle after learning the lesson from those nocturnal mammals the bats.

Night in the tropics is far noisier than the day! The crushing heat of day may silence even most of the birds. But once the sun has set, the tropical night, with little afterglow, falls quickly, and as if Nature had lifted a conductor's baton, the insect orchestra strikes up with horrible din. Millions of tree crickets and katydids raise their monotonous, deafening chant, with tree frogs chiming in. In parts of the African tropics, lions (which are mostly nocturnal) shake the blackness with a roar that seems to come from all around you. In the South American tropics, howler monkeys may make the night hideous. Even in your sleeping room the geckos may keep you awake with sounds like loud, smoochy, unashamed kissing. Geckos are squat lizards which can run up the

walls and even walk on the ceilings. They do humans no harm; on the contrary, they devour countless bothersome insects. But they have too much to say about it.

Our temperate-zone nights are quieter only by contrast. Actually there is a lot to be heard if you know what to listen for. There are the drummings of the ruffed grouse, the nighttime singing of the sweet little vesper sparrow, the moonlight sonatas of mockingbirds if you live down South or in California, and the whippoorwills all over the eastern states, especially in Dixie. One whippoorwill far in the distance has a sweet, lonesome, almost sleep-bringing quality. Two whippoorwills is one too many. Three may murder sleep.

The noisiest place in a temperate-zone night is not the forest (as in the tropics) but the neighborhood of a marsh. In spring there is the insistent *pe-yee-yeep!* of the spring peeper frogs, and the sound of the swamp tree-frogs—*creak, drack, crick*—like winding up a slow, noisy old clock. In summer the bullfrogs bellow their *deep,*

deep! and green frogs go *tung!* as if someone had plucked the deepest string on the 'cello. Add to this a lot of mysterious noises, plaintive whistlings and whinnyings, and sounds like a wooden razzle-dazzle or a paddle smacking on water. These are emitted by the various kinds of rail birds—the Virginia, sora, clapper, and yellow rails. Of all the common birds—for they really are common in cattail marshes, on salt marshes, along railroad ditches, even in the growth around a city park pond—rails are the least often seen, though they are about the noisiest. You see them only by accident, gumshoeing along on their rather short legs and clumsy feet, wearing a "who—me?" expression like somebody trying to sneak out of a room.

Of all the creatures of night the most magical are the fireflies, sometimes called lightning bugs. Indeed, lightning is a better word than fire for these little nocturnal beetles. For a fire burns steadily, whereas lightning flashes; a fire gives off heat, but the heat of a lightning flash cannot be felt if it doesn't strike you. And the magic of the fireflies' fire is that it gives out no heat—or none that can be felt by the human skin. You can catch one of these slow-flying beetles with a swoop of your hand (they don't bite or sting) and their little abdomens where they carry their torches feel cooler than the summer night air itself. Our most efficient electric light bulbs can put only 30 per cent of the current's energy into illumination; the other 70 per cent all goes into useless heat. Lightning-bug light is almost 100 per cent illumination. If you will put several lightning bugs under a glass tumbler, you will find they give enough light to read a newspaper by.

Why does the firefly carry a lantern around with him? He can't use it to find his way, for the light-producing organs are behind him, in the last segments of the abdomen. The light makes him more, not less, conspicuous to the toads which catch him by shooting out their long sticky tongues. Apparently the only purpose of the little wink is as a signal between the sexes. The male of one of our common fireflies flashes, as a rule, every five and eight-tenths seconds. From the grass the female signals answer. Hers is a weaker light, but all the same she is a bright girl, for she answers the male's signal exactly two and one-half seconds after she sees it. He flies down to her, signaling and guiding himself by her responses, till in the dew and darkness he finds his glowing mate. If you are enough of a mischief-maker to interfere with the course of true love, you may be able to trick the males into coming to you. Place a flashlight in the grass and turn it on, and quickly off, every two seconds, and you may bring the little suitor to your hands.

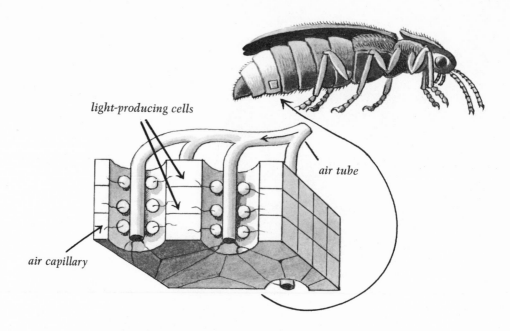

light-producing cells

air tube

air capillary

The firefly can withhold his flashing for a bit just as you can hold your breath, and if he is stunned by being knocked down and out of the air, he may do this. But if stimulated by fright or the presence of other males sharing his captivity, his flash may come faster just as you breathe faster if you are frightened or angry. You'll notice that even when not sending forth this beacon the lower abdomen of the firefly softly glows. For there lie the light-giving organs, made up of two layers of body tissue. The layer nearest the outside consists of fine grains, while the lower layer is composed of crystal cells which act as reflectors. Through the grains run air tubes as well as nerves. When the firefly feels an impulse to flash, the nerves command the air tubes to open wide. Then a rich supply of oxygen rushes over the grains so that they flare up in the lightning bug's flash of lightning, just the way a red ember of coal flares into fire if you give it a blast from the bellows.

Tropical countries can boast of more brilliant fireflies than ours. In the West Indies, the native Negroes sometimes tie them to their toes to show them the way at night through the undergrowth.

Brazilian girls put them in their hair to be glamorous. On the island of Jamaica great clusters of certain fireflies are so vivid that the palm leaves seem bathed in sheets of eerie fire. And in Siam the male fireflies cluster on the mangrove trees along the rivers, and flashing 120 times a minute, they sometimes fall into a regular rhythm, synchronizing their flashes. The result is that one moment there is blackness, and the next, every mangrove leaf, every houseboat on the river, every pagoda in the city, stands out as in a flash of lightning. Then blackness, then light, then blackness, then light—120 times a minute. What fairy fireworks!

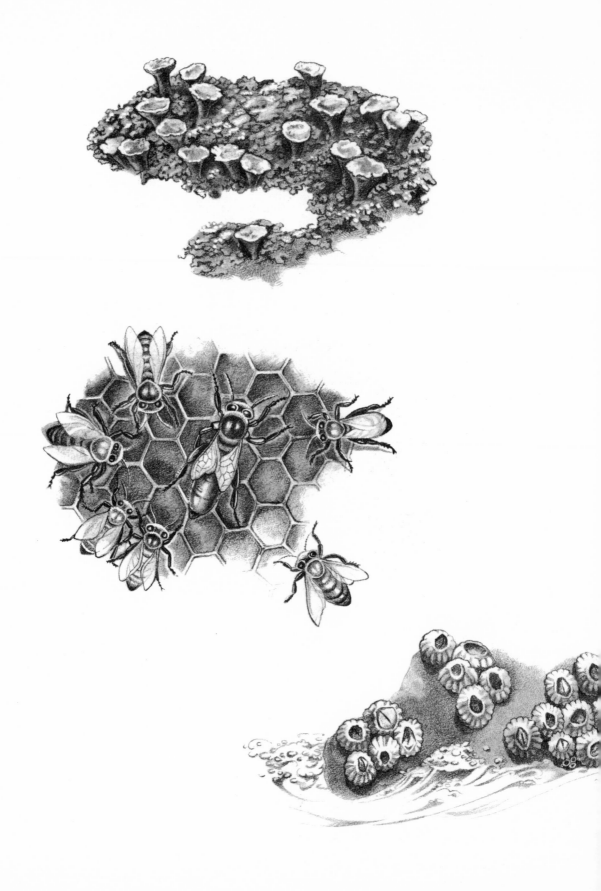

VI.

LIVING

TOGETHER

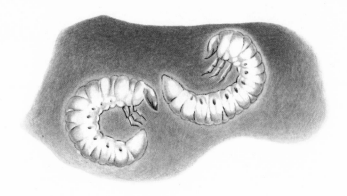

ANIMAL PARENTS

SOMETIMES it may seem to you that things in this world are all arranged for the convenience of grownups. But the truth of it is that *you* come first. You count most, you and all the other up-and-coming young things. Not only are you more important to your parents than anything else on earth, but throughout all Nature her first concern is for the future of the race, as embodied in you, in the cub, the kitten, the fawn, the grub, the very egg.

The instinct to protect and provide for the young is one of the oldest and strongest and strangest in life. Mother-love is a beautiful and familiar form of it. But creatures unable to feel this emotion perform the most complex and devoted acts for the sake of their offspring, sometimes when they are never even going to

see them. The cabbage butterfly unfailingly deposits her eggs upon cabbages (or plants of that family) without being able to have any tender notions of the caterpillars that will come out of the eggs and happily begin to eat the cabbage leaves. The Mayfly, although it cannot remember its own young days down in the

pond, drops its eggs in the water, the only place where they could succeed. And there is one creature, a solitary wasp, which goes hunting food for her offspring even before she has produced any. She first digs a hole and then sets out to seek a particular kind of insect which will form a healthful diet for a wasp larva. When she finds it, she does not kill it but instead stings it in such a way that it is paralyzed. Having thus provided meat that will stay fresh, she stores it in the hole, lays her egg upon it, fills up the hole and flies away. She never comes back to see how the egg is getting along,

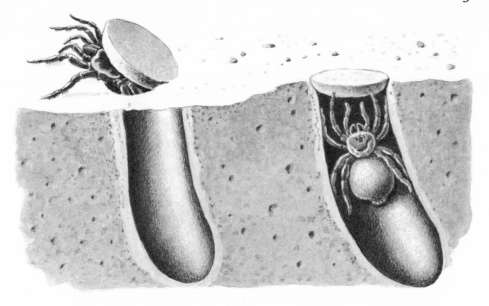

and if she is later shown the larva she appears indifferent to it. So you could not say that the wasp felt any maternal affection. Instinct alone, that great unreasoning force which drives so many living things toward success, has directed her how to care for her young blindly.

Your mother probably likes to know your whereabouts most of the time; she feels safer about you. That kind of parental anxiety can be found all through the animal kingdom, even in spiders. A spider keeps her eggs in a little silk bag she has made, and this bag is likely to be an object of great concern to her. In some species, she carries it with her everywhere, under her body attached by silken threads. In others, she leaves it in a safe place, sometimes hidden under bark or even inside leaves that she has bound together with her silk. The trap-door spider makes a hole in the ground and a lid for it with a hinge of silk; even with her eggs safe inside she may remain on guard, sometimes holding the trap door shut.

This concern for that most precious of treasures, the eggs, is shown even by cold-blooded creatures. And here it is often the father who appears more devoted than the mother. The male of a kind of toad called nurse toad or midwife toad carries the eggs in strings coiled about his hind legs until they are ready to hatch. The quaint little sea horse father takes the eggs about with him in

a sort of vest pocket. And it is the male of the stickleback fish that is the more earnest of the two parents. First of all he builds a nest out of bits of carefully chosen weed held together by a cement which he makes out of a secretion of his kidneys. When the nursery is ready, he goes out to find a lady stickleback who is heavy with eggs and coaxes her to come and lay them in his nest. When it is full of eggs, and he has fertilized them, he stays at the nest for nearly a month, defending it fiercely, changing the position of the eggs as seems necessary, and keeping a flow of fresh water bathing them by fanning with his fins and tail. Some fishes, like the male bowfin, keep as careful a watch over the young when they are hatched—even if the school numbers a thousand or more youngsters—circling around and above them as they explore the waters. Others take the baby fishes right into their mouths for protection when danger threatens and spew them out again when the coast is clear.

Perhaps these male fishes feel something you could call father-love. Certainly in birds parental care is tireless, courageous, and sometimes ready to sacrifice life itself. If that isn't love, I don't know what is. Building the nest is a job, and sitting on the eggs takes patience, but to keep the ravenous nestlings fed is almost

more than the poor parents can manage. One scientist in England, watching a pair of titmice, counted that in one day they made more than 475 trips to the nest. Then the young have to be taught to fly and often provided with food thereafter till they are able to forage for themselves. Strong indeed must be the instinct that gets a bird family raised!

How precious an egg can be is shown by the behavior of the emperor penguins, those absurd big birds of the Antarctic that live on the ice all their lives and look as though they were always dressed for a formal dinner party. A female penguin lays but one

egg, and not all females succeed in laying any. Moreover, to incu-
bate an egg when you live on ice is not easy. The penguin solves
the problem by taking the egg onto the top of its feet, and cuddling
it into a brood spot, a warm cavity low down in its body covered
by overlapping feathers. But so few are the eggs available, and so
maternal the penguins, that they will take turns incubating one
egg, even getting into terrific scrambles and scrimmages over
whose turn it is next to cuddle the beloved treasure.

As a rule, the higher up in the scale of development the animal is, the longer its infancy and the more care it requires. So the mammals, which nurse their young, keep them close and sometimes long, in some cases carrying them about till they must become a great nuisance. A baby kangaroo in its mother's pouch must be a bother when it gets big. (Maybe you know the joke about the mother kangaroo who cuffed her little one, saying: "That will teach you to eat crackers in bed!") The mother opossum, a rather

weak-minded creature who faints dead away when she is frightened, at least has the patience to take her large family everywhere
with her, at first in her pouch and later riding about on her back.
And bats, which make devoted mothers, not only keep their little

ones clinging close to them all day while they hang in cave or
hollow tree, but when they fly forth in the dusk they carry the
babies with them, even when the weight is greater than that of the
mother herself.

Everybody who has ever been a child—and that's everybody—
can see that parental care in a spider or a kangaroo, a stickleback
or a monkey, is the very same thing as that to which he owes his
own life. It is perhaps the most powerful force in the world,
stronger even than the instinct of self-preservation. And out of it
have grown impulses of devotion much broader in their scope.
From living for their own families, some animals—like some people—have learned how to live for their community. Let's look at
one of the most amazing of these animal societies.

AUGUSTE FOREL

ANT CIVILIZATIONS

A N ELEVEN-YEAR-OLD Swiss boy named Auguste Forel made a discovery about ants that had been overlooked by the greatest scientists before him. The garden of his house was populated by many of these strange, busy little insects. "There were big ants, little ants, black, red, and yellow ants," Forel recollected in later life. And when the boy investigated their hills or nests, he saw many curious sights; he saw that there were ants with wings and ants without them, and that there were motionless white cocoons which, like nursery infants in blankets, were carried about by the adult ants as danger threatened or temperature changes affected the nest. He saw wars between ant tribes, and the raids of slave-making red ants that carried off the cocoons of the black ants. "Neither my mother nor I could tell what it all meant," Forel tells us.

Then his mother put into his hands a book by the greatest

authority on ants, Huber, who once had wanted to marry her. She had found the book much too difficult and dull, she confessed to Auguste, but her son did not. He devoured it, and because the subject so absorbed him he mastered even the technical words easily as a boy can when he is interested in a hobby.

With a new understanding of what he observed, he kept on using his sharp young eyes. And one day he noticed that inside the nests of the big black ants there were tiny passageways belonging to a different kind of ant, a minute yellowish species. Then he discovered that the tiny ants would dash out of their galleries and devour the brood or young of the big ants. They were so quick at it they seldom got caught, but if they were they would gang up on the black ants, biting like demons, in such numbers that they usually won. And they could always retreat into their passageways which were much too small for the black ants to enter, as a rat hole is too small for a cat.

Auguste searched Huber's book through for any mention of this strange situation. It simply wasn't in the book. Realizing that even a boy could find out something unknown to the greatest of authorities, Forel decided then and there to become "the historian of the ants." On this he spent his life, and the history he produced, over a thousand pages long, stands on my desk, filled with fascinating information. But not even Auguste Forel learned all there is to know about ants, or a half, or the tenth part of it. Another boy or girl, here and now, could make plenty of new discoveries about them.

For whatever part of the country you may live in, there are just as many and as interesting ants about you as ever Auguste found in his Swiss garden. You can tell the acrobat ant by the fact that when you make a gesture toward it, it raises up its abdomen (though it hasn't got a sting) till it almost stands on its head. Those

tiny red house-ants that you can barely see are Pharaoh ants—
fancifully so called because they might have been one of the seven
plagues sent against Pharaoh, in the Bible. The little brown ants
that live under sidewalks are called the pavement ants—inhabitants of our cities since ancient times. Closely related is the steam-
ship ant, which long ago picked up the habit of invading ships and
then going on shore leave in the ports of all the world. Very big and

stiffly moving are the carpenter ants which get into woodwork in houses and like termites riddle it with their tunnels. The mound-builder ants, which make hills on prairies and in the woods, create great ant cities sometimes four feet high and as wide in diameter; I have seen these thick around the Chicago airport, each mound containing as many citizens, perhaps, as there are people in Chicago itself.

Ants have been called the mankind of insects, because theirs are the most complicated societies on earth, except our own. And every ant, of the more than three thousand kinds in the world, belongs to his community and indeed could not live long away from it. These communities are many and different. The army ants of the tropics are fierce, flesh-eating nomads that move about in a compact horde, carrying their babies and their queen with them; even lions and elephants flee before their terrible coming. Like a human army, these fierce marching insects can send out scouts to discover sources of food; they divide columns and flank to the right and left to make encircling movements. This is all the more astonishing because the army ants are absolutely blind; they communicate, like all ants, by scent and touch and also probably by sound.

Then there are harvester ants, which collect and store seeds, just like farmers. There are agricultural ants which grow crops— tiny toadstools whose spores they sow on fermented leaves kept in their nests underground. When a young female of such a nest goes off on her mating flight to found another colony, she takes some bits of the fungus with her to start a new crop in the new home. And there are dairy-farming ants, which keep other insects as men keep cows, especially the aphids that feed on plant juices; these the ants carry out every morning to pasture on our best flowers and fruit trees. The aphids suck the plant juices and, digesting

them, turn them into a sweet liquid called honeydew; the ants then "milk" their "cows" by stroking them till drops of the honeydew ooze out. Some ants even build "cow sheds"—leaves lightly glued or plastered down, under which the aphids are sheltered from the sun.

The great skill and co-operation of ants as engineers remind us still further of human civilization, for they can bridge chasms and cross water, tunnel earth sometimes down to nine feet, and even go through stone and masonry. Their wars and sieges with termites and honeybees and other kinds of ants are organized on a scale that finds no equal in the living world except among humans. Ants even keep and feed all sorts of useless pets—beetles and silverfish and other insects which you often see running along in ant columns. But, amazingly alike as they appear, the civilizations of ants and men are profoundly different at bottom. For ours is the result of intelligence, and that of ants is held together by instinct.

True that we have instincts and lively ones, like the instinct of self-preservation that saves our lives over and over before we have time to think what to do. Or the instinct to protect our young, even at the cost of our own lives. Falling in love is an instinct; when you come to do that, you won't need anybody to show you how! For that is the essence of instinct—that it knows what it needs to know without having to learn it. Indeed, instinct cannot learn; it knows nothing outside of itself. So ants, marvelous as they are in their complicated acts of co-operation, are really obeying instinct blindly; they are slaves to it. They cannot change the pattern of their civilizations as mankind constantly does.

And in these societies are various rigid classes of citizen. If you dig up an ant nest, you will find that there are several sizes of them, sometimes as many as four; the smaller ones do the lightest work and in case of battle are like light shock troops thrown into the fray in great numbers; the bigger ones you might call the heavy

troops, and in times of peace they do the harder work, such as cracking tough seeds with their great jaws. All the workers unite in guarding the eggs and feeding the tiny grubs; above all, every worker-soldier protects and feeds the queen, largest ant of all, who does nothing the year around but lay eggs.

Of these eggs the greater number will grow up to be members of the worker and soldier castes. But a few will turn out to be winged ants—the tiny males and the larger females or princesses, the future queens. Both the males and princesses are fed (they usually cannot feed themselves) and kept underground for safety until the temperature and season are just right. Then the workers bring

them up to the surface. For the first time they see the sunlight, and
they spread their tiny gossamer wings and take off into the sky.
When the marriage flight is over, the honeymooners come down
out of the bright air. The males, great numbers of them, die un-
mourned. Very different is the fate of the princess, who is a princess no longer but a queen. When she comes down to earth, her
first act is one that fills me with amazement each time I see it. She
deliberately pulls off her own beautiful fairy wings, and becomes
earth-bound. She now hates and fears sunlight as much as she
loved and sought it on her wedding flight. So she scrambles about
nervously till she finds a dark place to start her new family-city.

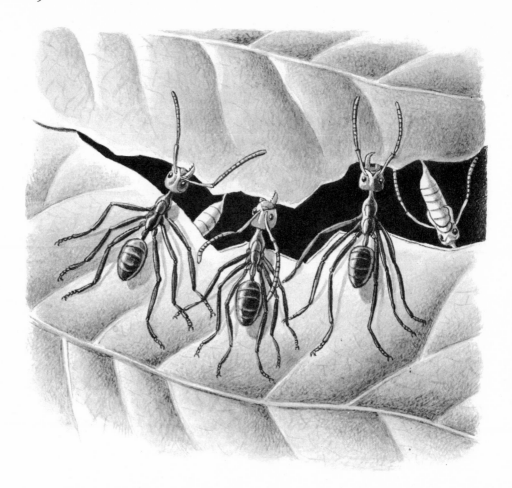

Each kind of ant has its favorite conditions; some burrow in the ground, some in the rootstocks of tropical ferns. Some live in rotted logs, and some make nests by stitching or gluing leaves together. Wherever a new queen nests, the rest of her life will be spent in laying eggs and being guarded and fed by her own daughters. We call her queen, but she is also a prisoner to the life of the community, a super-slave of the blind tyrant, instinct.

For freedom is something the ants know nothing about. Indeed, they exhibit strange and particular kinds of slavery one to another. When one species of ant raids another's nest for slaves, the raiders do not carry off adult ants, but instead they kidnap the youngsters in their cocoons and raise them up as their own. When these future slaves come out of their cocoons, they at once fall to work, as instinct commands them to do, tending their masters' young, defending the nest—even going on slave raids against their own kind to bring in more cocoons. The idea of rebellion never enters their heads because no idea of any sort ever enters there. Instinct alone is really master, and strangely does it rule one kind of ant called the shining amazon. This species has no workers at all, only males, females, and a ferocious soldier caste. They are all utterly helpless about making a nest of their own or even putting food in their mouths, and for such tasks they depend absolutely upon slave ants of other tribes. The more you study the wonderful and mysterious civilization of the ant peoples of the earth, the happier you can feel when you lift your eyes at last from their crawling, scurrying lives, and realize that you are an intelligent human being, free to make your own decisions.

ANIMAL AGGRESSORS AND
PLANT NOMADS

Now the ants that I watch in my garden are not the same ants which led their complex lives here in the days of the gentle Indians who first inhabited my California coast. Instead, they are Argentine ants, foreigners from South America which have come to dominate the scene and drive out the native species that are to be found only if I go up in the mountains to look for them. Just so is my garden invaded by snails with a destructive taste for my pansies; these too were introduced from Europe by some Frenchman who thought that snails made a delicious dish for dinner. (*I* think they taste like bits of old rubber tire!)

For the animal and plant population of this world is in a con-

tinuous state of shift. In the beginning of things, before adventur-
ous man began to sail the seas and cross the continents and tamper
with existing arrangements, Nature through the ages had worked
out a scheme of things that remained in a fairly stable balance.
But humans have interfered with this so many times that the
world has never been the same, nor is it so from year to year.

Many of the plants and animals come as stowaways in the bal-
last of ships, in shipments of fruit or other produce of foreign
places. Many others are introduced by some well-meaning soul
who thinks that he can improve on Nature. Once in a while the
idea proves successful, and the newcomer is welcome and a gain
to his new home. More often, the balance of Nature is so upset that
it never recovers, and the new addition becomes a pest requiring
large sums and great efforts to control it.

Most familiar example of the unwanted introduction is the English sparrow. About a hundred years ago an impulsive gentleman
decided that this country—so marvelously rich in beautiful and
tuneful native birds—would be improved by the house sparrow
common abroad, an ugly and unmusical little urchin of the city
streets. So about one hundred sparrows were imported and released in Brooklyn. They were expected simply to eat up some of
the wormy little grubs that were devouring the foliage of local
park trees. They did eat the grubs; they also ate everything else
they could find—seeds, young vegetables, useful rather than harmful insects; they settled right in with us, nesting in roof gutters and
stopping them up. They fought all the other birds, ganging up on
one pair at a time, then another. They ousted the house wrens
from the boxes put up for them; they drove the helpful and handsome house martins out of the martin houses many people raised.
When not fighting native birds, they quarreled with each other.

Their discordant chatter in the inner courts of city buildings was re-echoed and megaphoned by the stone well of the courts till everyone was sick of it. With incredible speed, they multiplied and spread all over the country, from Canada to Florida and out to California. They became the common bird of alleys and freight yards, where they lived like hoboes among the boxcars, picking up fallen bits of grain. They even settled in Death Valley as soon as men made their first settlements there.

For years it was thought impossible to keep down this dusty, dingy little ruffian of the streets, but his numbers have at last somewhat diminished. And one of the causes was another bright idea of the gentleman who introduced the sparrow; he also imported and released in our midst the European starling—an even tougher feathered customer, which drives out the sturdy sparrow.

These glistering black birds, which walk with a strut rather than

hopping and like to go about in great flocks, have become a terrible nuisance in some of our cities. At night they roost in tremendous numbers on the ledges and cornices of buildings, making a rusty, squeaky racket and a great deal of filth. In vain do the desperate citizens of New York or Washington try to rid themselves of the starling pests by traps, poison, fire hose, or noise makers. Starlings never know when their welcome is worn out.

Perhaps the most disastrous introduction of an alien ever made was that of the rabbit into Australia. It came as a Christmas present, on December 25 in 1859—twenty-four innocent-looking, large-eyed, long-eared bunnies. But rabbits multiply rapidly into astronomical figures. Six years after those two dozen were liberated on an estate west of Melbourne, the owner of the property killed twenty thousand! And the ones that got away kept on multiplying —and eating. They ate the bark of trees, thus killing them; they ate any seedling that dared to sprout; they ate the best grasses in

the pastures. And Australia lives largely by the sheep that depend on that pasturage. There are some hundred million sheep in Australia—and to every sheep, it is estimated, three rabbits!

Desperate have been the attempts to halt the destructive rabbit horde. Trapping and poisoning were tried in vain; hundreds of thousands of miles of fencing were built to hold back the advancing bunnies. Still they came, working their way throughout the southern two-thirds of that great continent. Cats, foxes, weasels were also imported by the thousands to combat the rabbits. The cats and weasels much preferred the native birds and small mammals, and left the rabbits alone. The foxes went after the lovely black swans and chased the kangaroos till the babies fell out of their mothers' pouches. There are still more rabbits in Australia than anyone could manage to count, and the cost of them can be figured in hundreds of millions of pounds.

It is dangerous to trifle with anything so free and strong as wild

life. True that some introduced species are welcome; we are glad to have the ring-necked pheasant in our fields, a handsome game bird originally from China but long a dweller too in England. The Hungarian partridge is also loved by the sportsman; it was first

brought to our shores by the son-in-law of Benjamin Franklin. It might have been pleasant to have had our skies spangled with the song of skylarks and our nights made romantic by the throbbing notes of nightingales, but neither of these species flourished when they were released here. And in New Zealand, where the skylark did succeed, it is now counted a pest!

For even apparently harmless animals can by their excess cause disaster. When goats multiply too freely and roam like wild things over the countryside, they are apt to eat everything growing, down to the roots, till the land becomes eroded and useless. True that Rikki-tikki-tavi, the mongoose of India, is a valiant snake killer. But he has also a taste for birds, and in Jamaica, where he

was brought to catch rats, he has sadly depopulated the lovely island of its feathered singers.

Some of the most destructive aggressions have been by silent, stealthy plant invaders. If Australia ever had a pest great enough to class with the rabbits, it was the prickly pear. This unfriendly kind of cactus, native only to the New World, was brought to New

South Wales in 1839, just one single plant of it. By the end of the century, it covered ten million acres, rendering them useless for grazing. Now you can't trap a cactus, nor set an animal to eat it up—it's too spiny to be appetizing to most creatures. But the scientists who specialize in biological control searched for an answer to the problem and found one. This was the caterpillar of a tiny moth from Uruguay. They sent a shipment of its eggs to the cactus-stricken country, and the caterpillars got to work as soon as they were hatched, eating out the fleshy stems of the cactus so that fungi and decay could complete their destruction. The conquest of the prickly pear by the caterpillar was a great victory, though you will not find it in your history books.

In Argentina the greatest plant curse of the pampas came from Europe—the milk thistle, a plant with leaves so veined with white that they look as if milk ran there. It is usually a low-growing, not too abundant, weed, but there come to the pampas great "thistle years," described to us by the naturalist W. H. Hudson in his book about his boyhood there, *Far Away and Long Ago.* Immense numbers of thistles sprang up and grew like Jack's beanstalk, shooting up to ten feet high. The gauchos, or cowboys, could scarcely see over the thistle tops even on horseback and had to keep to narrow cattle trails to get through them. The women in the ranch houses saw from their windows only thistles, like a Sleeping Beauty forest surrounding them. Then, as summer came on, the thistles all died. They became dry as paper, and one spark from a cigarette was enough to start a raging fire. Animals and gauchos alike fled before it, and only when thunderstorms broke at last were the fires extinguished. Men and animals once more went abroad freely, for the hated thistles were gone—until next time.

Our own country was invaded in 1875 by a prickly aggressor

native to Siberia. It came, in the form of stowaway seeds, in a shipment of flax seed imported to South Dakota from Russia. There it had already driven out every farmer in large areas by its cruel spread. For this Russian thistle forms great prickly balls of vegetation that no growing animal cares to touch. When it dies at summer's end, this ball breaks free of the dead root and rolls away before the wind. As it jumps like a jack rabbit and tumbles like a circus clown, it drops its slim and shining seeds, forever conquering new territory. So within twenty years of its arrival, it had spread over sixteen of our states and ten provinces of Canada.

A relative of this thistle that grows wild on the alkaline desert

steppes of southeastern Russia has more recently penetrated our western states, bringing disaster. This plant, called halogeton, got a foothold in northeastern Nevada where it felt at home on the alkaline soil and found much of the ground left bare from overgrazing by sheep. It began to spread, and the sheep began to die. Not for some time could the sheepmen pin the murder on this plant with the spongy leaves that turn purplish in autumn when the other browse is dying off. Nor have they been able with fire or weed killers to halt the death march of halogeton, which has spread over most of Nevada, much of Utah, and even into Montana. The best likelihood of stopping it would be to stop overgrazing and give the native range grasses a chance to fight back.

Most of the plants we call weeds have come to us thus from the Old World, slipping in unnoticed to flourish by reason of their sturdy coarseness. You'll remember that in "Hiawatha" the Indians speak of the common plantain as "the white man's foot" because it seemed to spring up everywhere that our race first walked. Some of these plant tramps have apparently lived with humanity from ancient times. In our American cities we see, in vacant lots, around railroad yards and docks and wharves, various kinds of pigweed and goosefoot, unsightly as rats or starlings and just as able to edge their way into our cities. When you look for their native homes where they are wild, you can't seem to find them. In Europe I saw them growing only where they do in America. They seem to have been city and barnyard weeds since ancient times, and probably they flourished in the alleys of Babylon, while Babylon still stood.

But in the great influx of plants and animals from other countries much has come that enriches our own. Of the cereals that are the staff of life, only corn is native here; it was grown by the Indians long before history began. Wheat, rice, barley, oats, and

the rest come to us from other lands, as in great measure do our fruits, our shade trees, our flowers, our domestic animals. Once foreigners among us, they are now naturalized and valued citizens. For better or worse, the day of a perfectly balanced, purely native Nature is over. Instead, we have a vast international exchange, both accidental and by intent, of species all over the globe. Truly, this has become, for Nature as well as for mankind, one world.

THE WEB OF LIFE

All things by immortal power,
Near or far,
Hiddenly
To each other link'ed are,
That thou canst not stir a flower
Without troubling of a star.

THE poet who said that was putting a great scientific truth in an unscientific way. But beauty is exact in a way of its own, so that Francis Thompson swiftly conveys in these words a great and complicated meaning. He is talking about what scientists call the web of life, the marvelous inter-relation between all parts of Nature, the most distant as well as the most closely connected.

When you step out on a fine dewy morning and see a spider web glittering with the drops of the night and touch one of the strands of the web, every drop trembles; some will run together or fall. If the spider is present, she feels your touch and is apt to run and hide herself, or she may stick bravely to the center of the web. If you tear the web, she will wait till you are gone, or more probably

until nightfall, and then secretly repair it. Every strand is important to her.

All the living world is a web like that, and a touch upon it in one spot may make distant strands quiver. Over and over it is rent, here or there, and laboriously repaired. Wars, droughts, floods, famines make tears in our human fabric that anyone can recognize; none is more swiftly wrought than by one of the great hurricanes that may strike our coast. At once you see how the strands of our communication, for instance, are ripped away; telephone wires are down; bridges are washed out; busses stop running, and schools and offices may close. It takes days of hard work to get this interweaving repaired.

In Nature the pattern is not so immediately seen, but it goes even deeper, down to the bottom of life and all the way through it. To perceive this, you have only to look at the living world and think about it for a little. If you are on a walk in the autumn woods, for instance, sit down on a log and wait for the animals to forget you are there and take up their affairs again. The squirrels stop scolding at you, and go about their acorn-business. Scatterbrains that they are, they often forget where they bury their nuts, and so unwittingly plant many new trees. The woodpeckers, silenced by your rustling through the leaves, take up again their knock-knock-knocking. You may see one of them cock an ear against the side of the trunk to listen for the tunneling and chewing of the engraver beetle which makes destructive galleries in the wood just under the bark. When he hears it, he will thresh open a little hole, and the next minute the beetle larva is out of the tree and inside the woodpecker.

He is not the only good forester among the birds; countless little warblers are constantly gleaning the leaves and twigs for harmful insects, while the nuthatches and tree creepers search every crevice in the bark for leaf-eating caterpillars. And the birds which eat the sweet blue berries of the juniper, and then void the seeds, are tree-planters as carelessly helpful as the squirrels. In turn, the trees serve the birds which serve them, offering nesting sites as well as banquet tables. Thus do the lives of both animal and vegetable kingdoms interlock and merge.

In the autumn woods there steals to you that wonderful underground smell of damp earth and mushrooms, an odor a little sad with the dying year, yet delicious too. At your feet, the leaves of last year are being turned to mold by the action of harmless, hard-working soil bacteria. Thus they will make a rich loam in

which this year's crop of seeds will grow. Decay is not the end of things in Nature; it often forms a new beginning. So that dead tree above you has its uses; in the hollow, eaten out of its trunk by wood-destroying fungi, a pair of owls have a nest. As each stone in a cathedral not only supports the stones above it, but itself contributes to the grand design of the whole, so in a natural scene like a wood there is an almost architectural balance. Each species lives there in its own niche because no other could fill that particular place so well.

Nothing shows the interdependence of living things more curiously than the fungi that fill the autumn woods with their secretive odor. After the first rains, they spring up impishly everywhere, as though at the wave of a wand. A few are poisonous, and so nobody should eat wild mushrooms who is not an expert on them, for there is no easy and shorthand way to tell a dangerous toadstool from a harmless mushroom. All hide their secrets in quaint and fantastic forms. Some fungi look like frail clumps of coral, others like the bearskin shakos worn by the guards at Buckingham Palace. Some take the form of shelves or brackets coming

out of the tree trunks, and some that are found on fallen twigs look like trembling slices of wine jelly. There are little elf cups growing on crooked stems, and other kinds like bits of sponge. On the ground you may find earthstars or, if you have sharp eyes, a fungus that looks like a minute bird's nest, even to the cluster of tiny "eggs" at the bottom.

Fungi come in strange and lovely colors. There are scarlet- and orange-capped toadstools, and others that are a royal violet, shading down to the most delicate tints of pink and pale lavender and the mother-of-pearl tones of human flesh—and finally to the

corpse-like and waxen perfection of a kind called the destroying angel, which does indeed bring death if it is eaten. But there is one color that you never see in a fungus, and that is the green pigment of chlorophyll found in the leaves of plants that make their own food. For the fungi cannot do this. Lacking chlorophyll, they have to find other ways of getting nourishment. And these are wondrously interbraided with the lives of other things.

Some fungi get their food from green living plants; these are the parasites. The conch fungus, one of the bracket kind shaped rather like a shell, is hated by lumbermen because it destroys healthy timber. It sends its suckering fine strands into the wood and robs the tree of much nourishment, doing no service in return. But other fungi—and these form the greatest number—live on wood already dead, or on the dead leaves of the forest floor. These are not parasites but saprophytes, and they do no harm but only a great good, turning outworn materials back into fertile earth mold, to be used all over again by growing things. In the web of life, theirs is a thread that weaves the dead back into the pattern of the living.

Yet some fungi live so intimately with other organisms that both of them benefit. This kind of mutually helpful relationship is called a symbiosis. It is a very particular kind of living together, not a mere happenstance neighborliness or an incidental usefulness to one another, but an interdependence in which two very different kinds of living thing are actually necessary to each other. Fungi have a symbiotic relation with some ferns, with a number of wild flowers like wild ginger and Indian pipes, with heather and heath, and above all with certain orchids. These will not even flower without their secret partner, fungus. And the strands of the fungus may extend right into the tiny orchid seeds, which are

as fine as grains of sand, so that when the seed blows away it takes a minute quantity of fungus with it. When it sprouts, its strange ally starts to grow right up with the little plant. You couldn't find the web of life knotted more tightly than in such an orchid.

Even the pines and oaks, larches and spruces, birches and beeches that stand in such noble independence throughout the woods have a friendly partnership sometimes with the toadstools quaintly snuggled at their roots. These fungi may grow so intimately with a tree that they send their strands far up in its tissues and out into the soil beyond its roots. These strands, very thin-walled, are more efficient at taking up soil water than the roots of the tree itself. So the tree benefits immensely from its little fungus guest. True that the guest takes a trifle of the food manufactured by the leaves of its great host. But this is a case where "fair exchange is no robbery." An amanita toadstool, its bright red cap like a warning of poison, growing at the foot of an old oak, is partner to it, connected by fine subterranean threads. Yet, were you to eat it, it would be the end of you. We cannot call the amanita good or bad, for these are not words that can be used about Nature. We can only remember that we all have our own places in it, and that vast and shining is the web of life, trembling at any touch, yet enduring forever.

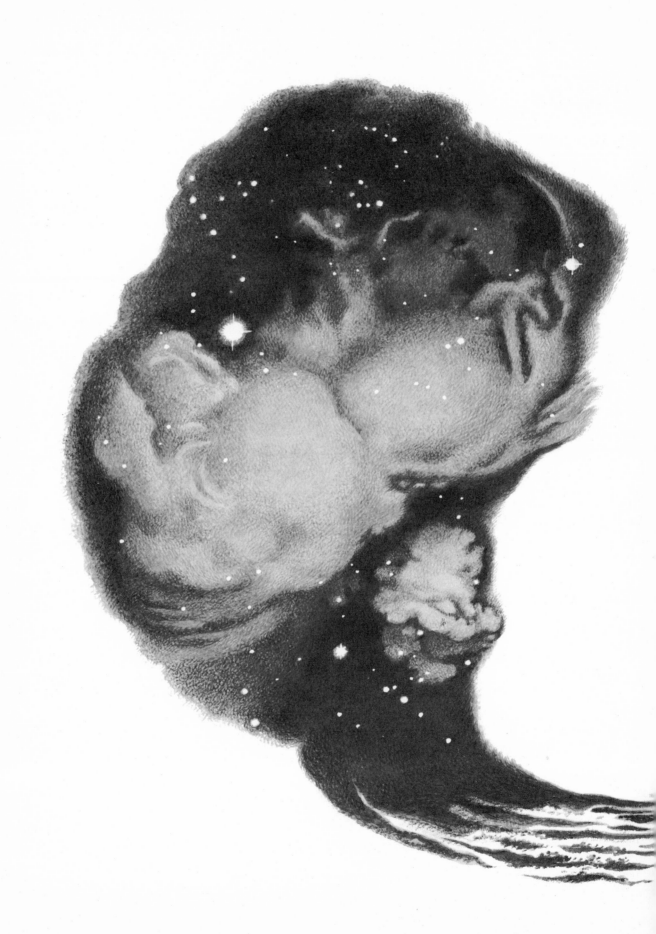

VII.
THIS
EARTHLY
HOME

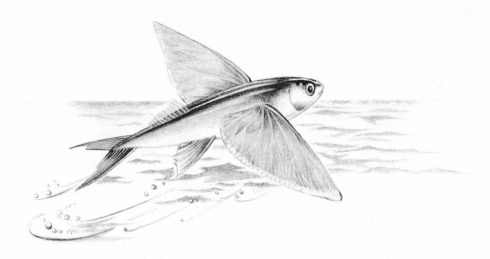

DOWN, DOWN, DOWN!

WE HAVE all read in science fiction about journeys to other planets which are supposedly inhabited by intelligent beings who pit their hostile wits and machines against ours. Sometimes there are descriptions, too, of the natural history of these imaginary worlds, weird plants and weirder animals. It makes amusing reading, but that is all such stories were ever intended to be—amusing. At least as far as the parts about other-planetary life are concerned, it is just guesswork. And guesswork is not part of science.

For life is possible only under certain conditions and these are not found outside a very narrow range. Beyond these boundaries, death awaits every plant or animal. Some of our space-travel imaginers might argue that what I have just said is true only of life "as we know it" here on earth. But what is the use of discussing life as we *don't* know it? It is "just pretending" to change the rules and say that life might be possible on a planet that is molten hot, or one that has no oxygen and no water. You might also say that on some other planet football is played where the goal posts are at opposite ends of Infinity, where the ball, once kicked, travels out into space and never comes back, and the players, being rooted in stone, cannot leave their places. But it wouldn't be football any more, would it? So life, *as we know it,* is all the life there certainly is!

And we certainly know the rules of the great game of life here on earth. Rule One says there must be free oxygen. It mustn't be locked away in chemical combinations with other elements such as iron (making iron rust) or carbon (making carbon monoxide). It must be available, pure, plentiful, for breathing.

Rule Two tells us that there must be water for growing. No water, no growth, says Nature sternly. The water necessary to support life must not be permanently frozen into ice nor exist only as water vapor or dampness or steam in the air. It must be nice, wet, liquid water that plants and animals can drink and grow on.

Rule Three brings in light, not only as a source of heat but as the main (indeed almost the only) source of energy for the world of living things.

And, last of all, Rule Four says that the temperature on any planet that supports life must be regulated within certain limits. The temperature mustn't fall permanently below the freezing point of water. And it mustn't rise, even for a few minutes, to the boiling point of water.

Now if you apply these four rules to this planet home of ours, the Earth, you'll find that the region where life is possible is such

a thin film that if the planet were a stack of books as high as twenty-five volumes of the encyclopedia, the habitable or life-supporting part would be represented by the thickness of one page!

Let's look at the situation: Our planet has a radius (from the surface to the center) of about four thousand miles. But there are only about twenty-four inches of soil that are really teeming with life—most of it soil bacteria, earthworms, millepedes, and the grubs of insects and fine threads of fungi. Roots of trees may go down fifty feet or more, but this is exceptional and the real life of a tree is led above ground, not below.

True that mankind has sunk some very deep mines—a mile and a half down in South Africa where the search for gold has made it worth while to dig so deep. But the heat set up by the pressure of the rocks is so great there that five minutes' work seems to the miners like five hours. Even with fresh air forced into the shafts, life is hard to sustain there. Poisonous and inflammable gases constantly collect in such mines. Only the rats and the fungi that destroy the mine timbers seem to flourish in this underworld.

Naturally the ocean is a much better place for life at great depth. Water allows the sunlight to penetrate it, not so well as air, but far better than does the soil. And sunlight, of course, is a necessity for the plant growth on which all life depends, in the sea as it does on the land. Most seaweeds grow only where they can root on the ocean floor and still receive sunlight. The one-celled diatom plants, which are the grass or pasturage of the sea, can float freely, so they may be found living far from shore and at all the depths where light still shines.

But the sunlight in sea water changes its quality as it sinks. The red rays are the first to be absorbed and disappear. As a result, the many kinds of fish, squids, and other marine life which appear as red when brought to the surface, would be black, and hence almost invisible, in the depths. This camouflages them quite well, either for attack or defense.

At about fifteen hundred feet, all the green disappears from sea water, as Dr. William Beebe, the famous American scientist, found when he descended in the clear waters off Bermuda in his steel ball with windows, called the bathysphere. The underwater world at this depth was thus completely blue, and the color lingered eerily even when it was too faint to illuminate the passing fishes. At 3,038 feet, Dr. Beebe reports, all visible light disappeared. There was total darkness except when some luminous fish, like a firefly of the sea, went by, or when he switched on a powerful electric searchlight that shone out of his window into the eternal night of the deep.

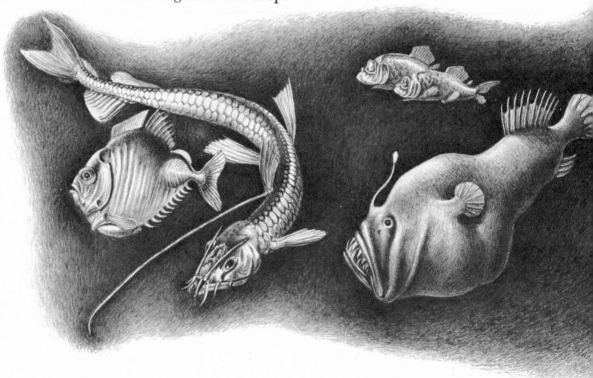

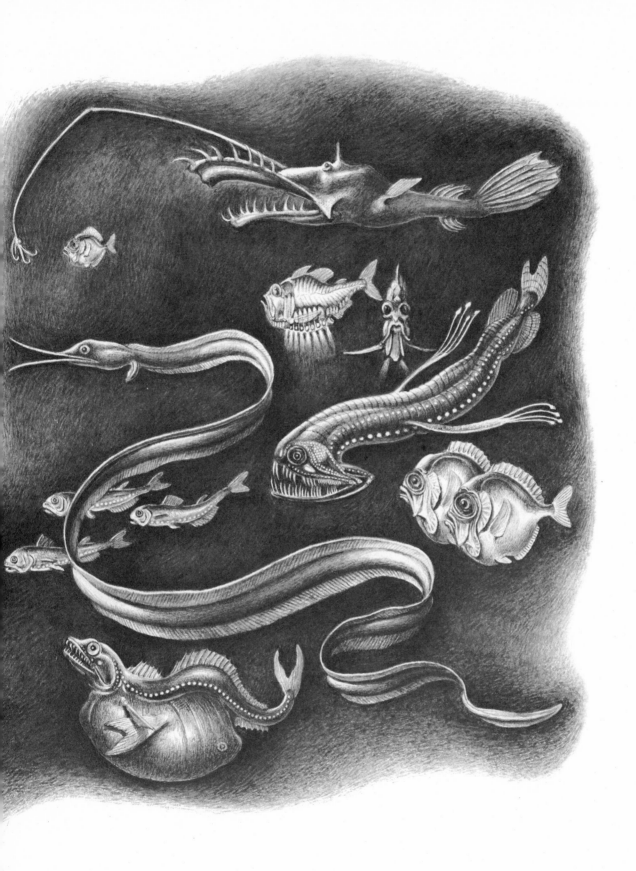

These deep-sea creatures take on forms so fantastic that it was hard for Dr. Beebe to believe his eyes, and it is hard, too, for us to believe even the evidence of his camera. Usually their bodies are very small in proportion to their big heads. But their heads are not occupied by extra brains but by vastly gaping mouths armed with horrible fangs, and with enormous eyes fit for seeing in the dark.

Now what, you may ask, can creatures in that pitchy and eternal blackness expect to see? They see each other's various lights, for a large proportion of these deep-sea creatures are luminous. The finger squid carries two bulb-like orange lights on its longest arms. Creatures that snap at these lures, thinking they are the lights of small edible fish, find themselves seized by muscular tentacles with sucking disks and brought to the squid's mouth. The angler fish carries its own fishing rod—a long flexible stalk of cartilage rising from its forehead. At the end is a grapnel with three sharp hooks, each with a yellow light on it. Anything so unwary as to snap at this bait finds itself firmly hooked, and in a few moments inside the angler fish's stomach.

Drifting through the deeps go millions of creatures tiny as insects, often brilliantly colored and also luminous. They are copepods and isopods, minute relations of shellfish, and together they are called the "krill." These bug-small living things feed on even smaller ones, those microscopic plants, animals, and plant-animals that, sinking down and down after death in a slow perpetual rain, form the queerly named oozes at the very bottom of the ocean. On the krill itself feeds many a deep-sea swimmer; indeed, the largest of all, some of the great whales, live on nothing else.

Other whales, in pursuit of bigger and juicier food, have been known to sound down to one mile below the surface. That is the extreme lower limit for any mammal in the world. Life in other forms is fairly abundant at two miles down. But remember that in some places the ocean is seven miles deep! And very few living things have ever been dredged up from those awesome, farthest pits of the sea.

THE SKY IS THE LIMIT!

As we follow life up the high mountains of this world, we find that it grows both sparser and, as in the depths of the ocean, stranger. The trees get smaller and smaller until presently you are taller than they are. Lashed by winds, bent by the loads of snow that lie on them most of the year, they crouch along the ground, so that you can sometimes walk on the tops of their stiff, gnarled, closely set branches. At last the trees give up entirely. You are now above timber line and up in the alpine meadows. Far below you, swim the misty blue-green valleys; above you, not very far, hang glaciers and snow fields that go to the top of the mountains or, if the topmost crags are too steep to hold their snow and ice, give place to barren pinnacles of rock bleak above the snow line.

Here in the alpine meadows, if it is summer down below, the brief spring is just coming. Wide-eyed wild flowers star the short turf, brilliant in the clear light. Their stems are often very short and their leaves all lie in a little rosette flat on the ground as though they hugged it for warmth. The blossoms of blue gentians and yellow eyebrights and rose campions seem surprisingly big by contrast with their dwarfed stems. For all the chilly air, they have plenty of insect visitors. Bumblebees, protected by their dense hairy coats against the sharp winds, buzz noisily everywhere in the carpet of flowers, tumbling and guzzling them in their thirst for sweet nectar, but also accomplishing their pollination. Many alpine butterflies, too, flit from bloom to bloom.

In the Alps, you hear skylarks spangling the air with twittering song. In the high Sierra Nevada of California, marmots, those jolly-looking burrowing rodents, whistle clear as bird song. Life in an alpine meadow, if you come in summertime on a fine day without too much wind, seems paradise. You wonder why anyone would ever want to leave this pure, exhilarating air, this clean, noble, lofty scenery. You forget that for most of the year, icy, howling winds whip these high places with a cruel lash.

Yet really this world of gentians and bumblebees isn't so very high, after all. Atop the greatest mountain ranges of the world, such as the terrifying Andes or the still more awesome Himalayas of Central Asia, the air is so thin—that is, oxygen-deficient—that every breath you draw feels like your last one on earth. Oxygen is a heavy gas, and thus sinks to the bottom of our sea of air, so that the higher up you go the less of it there is. You have to work hard just drawing in enough to keep the red corpuscles of your blood nourished with it, and any other effort seems too much. I knew a boy of sixteen who climbed the Matterhorn, one of Switzerland's most magnificent peaks, while his sister watched him from the valley through a telescope. It was agreed between them that when he reached the top he was to wave a flag; at last she saw it flutter but did not see him fall down on his face, utterly exhausted just by the effort of lifting a banner weighing a few pounds.

Apparently Nature did not fit our bodies for existence at fifteen thousand feet. Children born at very high altitudes have a much higher death rate than normal. But if these high-born children survive at all, they develop extra big lungs and chest cavities to do the necessary hard breathing, and they accumulate extra supplies of red corpuscles; you'd have to say they were more red-blooded than the rest of us. People who are not used to such heights, when they come up swiftly from the lowlands, may develop mountain sickness. Even a little touch of it once made me feel that I wanted to lie down and die. I did lie down—but I didn't die, and in a couple of hours felt fine again!

Plenty of animals, however, are perfectly fitted for living in the high mountains. Though they cannot survive where the air is very thin, they are positively jumping and bounding with activity on terrible cliffs where human climbers crawl with pick, piton, grapple, alpenstock, and ropes. Later these mountaineers write books to tell us what a remarkable thing they accomplished—at which the wild sheep and goats of the mountains (if they could read) would bleat with laughter.

The chamois, an antelope of the Alps, has little hollow cups under its dainty hooves, which act like suction disks, so that he thinks nothing of a standing broad jump of twenty feet across a chasm and can land with all four hooves—and stop dead, without toppling—on a sloping ledge whose area is no bigger than your hand. The chamois flit across the face of a cliff that looks to us absolutely smooth and vertical; they leap up as boldly as they jump down, down, down to some invisible ledge. In all the great mountain systems of the world there are sure-footed creatures, mostly of the goat, sheep, antelope, rabbit, and cattle families, which can jump and climb, or walk over snow and ice without breaking through, and skip lightly over the very slides of broken rock that make humans lumber and scramble and stumble so clumsily.

Most of them, like the little chinchillas of the Andes, wear double coats of fur to keep them warm. The yak, a great, grunting ox of the Himalayas, has practically an overcoat over his regular fur one that swings shaggily to the ground; even the soles of his feet are fur-clad. The white ptarmigan birds of the high peaks have feathers on their feet, that look and work like snowshoes. So each alpine creature is just as well adapted to his high life as the deep-sea creatures to their existence in the heavy depths.

Here is a table of the highest points where various forms of animal life have been found in the Himalayas:

Marco Polo sheep	12,000	feet
highest human habitations	16,200	"
green toad	16,400	"
grasshoppers	16,470	"
Parnassius butterflies	17,000	"
men herding their flocks	18,150	"
wolves	18,480	"
argali (sheep)	19,140	"
mouse hare	20,000	"
yak	20,000	"
jumping spider	22,000	"
alpine choughs (crow-like birds) following humans up Mt. Everest	27,000	"
human climbers without oxygen tanks	28,000	"
top of Mt. Everest, reached with oxygen tanks by men (May, 1953)	29,140	"

Birds, of course, are not earth-bound like the rest of us at high altitudes. They are so light, even the mighty condors, that they can balance on the upward drafts of air and let themselves be shot up to great heights without having to flap a stroke. So it is not sur-

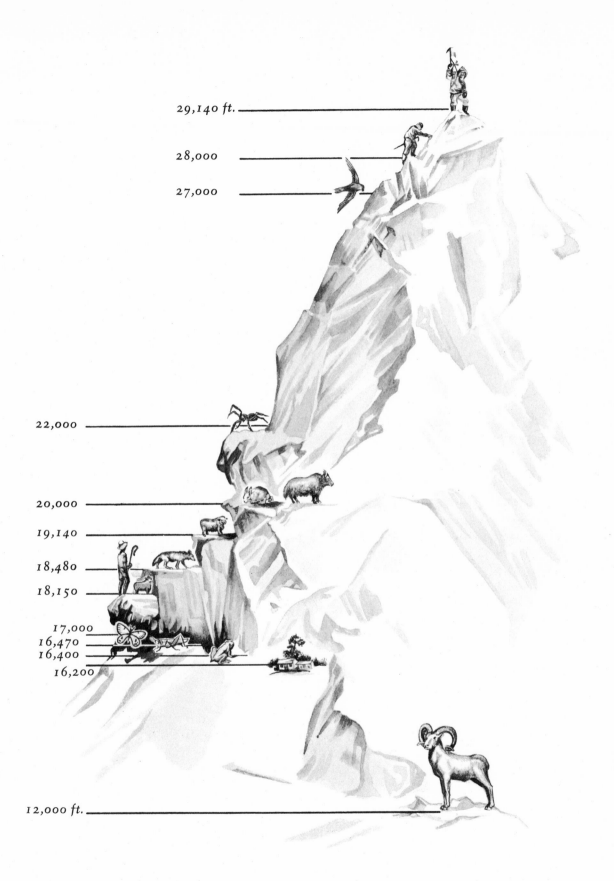

29,140 ft. _____

28,000 _____

27,000 _____

22,000 _____

20,000 _____

19,140 _____

18,480 _____

18,150 _____

17,000 _____
16,470 _____
16,400 _____

16,200 _____

12,000 ft. _____

prising to hear that the South American condor is seen in the air at twenty-three thousand feet, while on Mt. Everest climbers have observed vultures at twenty-five thousand feet—presumably waiting for somebody to die! Birds sometimes migrate, too, at great heights. Geese in India have been seen by plane pilots migrating at twenty-nine thousand feet, while in Egypt the beautiful Nile goose has been detected in migration at approximately thirty-five thousand feet. And this is up in the stratosphere.

For our sky is composed of layers or spheres. The troposphere is the layer lying nearest the earth, and it extends upward to 31,500 feet. The troposphere is the zone of clouds and winds, of storms, rain, snow, and fast and extreme changes of temperature.

It's where all the weather is and almost all the oxygen. By contrast, the stratosphere has practically no weather—no violent changes of temperature, no boisterous winds blowing this way and that, very few clouds, very little oxygen, and very low temperatures. In its cold stagnation and oxygen deficiency it greatly resembles the depths of the sea—with the differences, of course, that it is brilliantly lighted, and instead of a water pressure of seven tons per square inch, there is an air pressure of only one and six-tenths pounds. (Fourteen and seven-tenths is the pressure on every square inch of our bodies at sea level.)

Just as bold scientific explorers are always venturing farther into the depths of the sea, so the records for ascending into the stratosphere are repeatedly broken. It is found that as you go up and up, the temperature goes down and down. The sun in those cloudless realms shines like a blazing white searchlight, out of a practically black zenith. The oxygen content of the air, of course, is quite insufficient to support human life, and delicate instruments sent aloft even higher than men can go show that the stratosphere is constantly bombarded with a deadly rain of cosmic rays. The only life ever discovered at heights like ten or thirteen miles above the earth is the smallest and lightest we know. Bacteria, such as commonly live in the soil and certain spores—the seed-like reproductive cells of several kinds of mold—have been captured at these great altitudes on specially prepared sticky plates. How far these tiny vessels of life may float in space no one can say.

But it is here below, here on solid earth between the cold dark depths of the sea and the empty heights of the sky that the grand, lively, crowded pageant of Nature goes on. It passes forever, and is forever changing. In former times, in earlier ages, there were

countless species like the dinosaurs and mammoths which are
gone today. They have died out, become extinct, passed from the
busy scene. In the future there will appear, no doubt, new kinds
of plants and animals that we cannot now imagine, developed out
of changes in our present species. And some of the creatures and
flowers we know today will probably become extinct in their turn.
So this spinning globe we live on, this planet Earth, is like a stage
on which many plays have been acted, and many, many actors
have come, and gone. All things go. The miracle of life, the endless adventure, endures.

How did it all get started? Where did it come from? Where
does it go—this thing called life, which is like nothing else? The
end of this book brings us no nearer an answer than the beginning when these questions were first asked. Wherever it came
from in the beginning, life cannot be created out of anything but

the living. All the inventiveness of man, all the astonishing new materials and methods he is forever thinking up, cannot produce life. When it is gone, he cannot bring it back. The French scientist Pasteur, who taught us how to pasteurize our milk, was the first to show that when you kill all germs on, say, a surgical instrument, and then keep it in a sterile wrapping, it will never, never have a germ on it. Even bacteria, it seems, have to have ancestors. Even an Edison or an Einstein cannot make an oak tree. Only an acorn can do that.

So, indomitably, a million kinds of living things and more keep on coming, crowding this planet stage called Earth with color and form and animation. Here, and here only, is all of life we know. The astronomers who search the heavens with their telescopes and spectroscopes discover no spacemen, no flying saucers there; instead they find that the suns of outer space are too hot

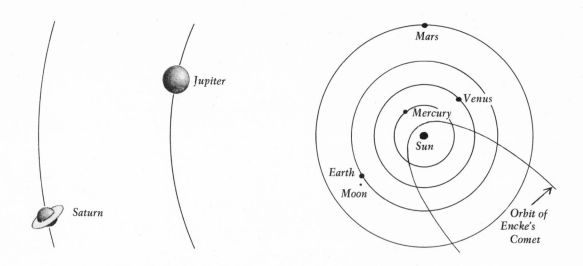

for life, the spaces between them too deadly cold, and that even here in our own solar system our sister planets are most unwelcoming to life. The outer planets are too far from the sun to receive its warmth, and those nearest it get too much heat. Little Mercury is so hot on the sun side that lead would melt there, and on the shady side it is always icy cold. Venus is wrapped in clouds that never lift, mysterious and unpromising. On Mars, the peering astronomers see green spots that may be vegetation. These increase in the Martian summer, and shrink back to the Martian tropics in winter. If plant life that is, then it must be very limited. For on Mars is little water vapor and less oxygen—not enough to keep a candle burning. And water and oxygen, life must have.

Only on the third planet from the sun, this Earth of ours, are things just right for living and growing and multiplying. Water we have in quantities; two thirds of the surface of our globe are covered with water. Slower to heat than land or air, it is also slower to cool, so like a mighty thermostat it keeps our planet home a comfortable temperature. Oxygen we have in plenty and in just the right mixture with nitrogen. And this atmosphere of ours lets through the healthiest of the sun's light and keeps out the deadlier rays.

The spinning of our planet on its axis, which gives us day and night, the tilting of our earth which gives us seasons, the winds which mix the air and bring us clouds and blow them by again —all go to make Earth, good old gusty, dusty, misty, and sometimes misbehaving Earth, the best place we know of in the universe to live. As it goes spinning around the sun, following in a spiral while the sun plunges through endless space, our world is something like Noah's ark, crowded with the animals. There is no mention in the Bible story of plants on board, but perhaps Noah took seeds of everything too. Anyway, we are all in it together, all on the great adventure, sharing the precious gift of life.

BOOKS FOR FURTHER READING

The books and articles mentioned below are just a few, out of a great number, that you may find on library shelves and in bookstores. Book titles marked with an (*) are written especially for readers about ages ten to sixteen. That doesn't mean that the other books are too difficult for young readers, for I have not listed any that are very technical. When the page numbers of magazine articles are followed by the Latin abbreviation *et seq.* ("and those following"), it means that the rest of the article is continued on various pages further on, just the way news columns are continued on back pages of a newspaper.

Books mentioned as being out of print are, of course, not obtainable from publishers or regular bookstores. But they can often be found on library shelves, and secondhand bookstores may have them, sometimes at nominal prices. It is surprising what a large number of expensive and beautiful books are on library shelves where you can consult them. And some of these old and out-of-print books are just as fine, or better, than some of the new books. So it is well worth your while to make a trip to the nearest library and find out what it has to offer you. Librarians are usually very helpful to people who show a genuine interest in some subject.

Magazine articles are also rich in information. Most libraries have files of *Natural History, Audubon Magazine, National Geographic, Nature Magazine, Reader's Digest, Life,* and *Holiday*. If you know the year and month, you can ask for any "number" of a magazine, and the librarian will be glad to show it if it is in stock. Secondhand bookstores, too, often have the number you want if you know what year and month to ask for.

To help you to use the following list, here is the plan of it, with headings and subheadings:

BIRDS

GENERAL BOOKS

(not including identification handbooks)

The Book of Bird Life, by Arthur A. Allen. 426 pages; photographs. $5. Van Nostrand. New York. 1930. A fine all-round book. Tells how birds live; gives history of ornithology, classification, distribution, and migration of birds, bird communities, courtship, home life, coloration, and camouflage; gives methods of studying and attracting birds; tells how to take bird walks, keep bird calendars, how to use observation blinds and to band birds; discusses birds as pets, bird photography, and bird songs.

Birds Over America, by Roger Tory Peterson. 342 pages; photographs. $2.95. Grosset & Dunlap. New York. 1953. A wonderful all-round book about a wide variety of bird life on sea beaches, in city streets, over the ocean, in the grip of hurricanes, told through the experiences of a leading ornithologist. City boys' bird clubs, champion-length bird lists, Christmas bird censuses, adventures with great birds of prey are among the absorbing topics taken up in this easy-to-read book.

Birds in the Garden and How to Attract Them, by Margaret McKenny. 349 pages; photographs, color plates. $3.95. Grosset & Dunlap. New York. 1948. Covers a wide range of topics in popular style: the economic side of birds, planting for birds, feeding devices, birdhouses, care of stray and injured birds, bird banding, birds in the city garden, photography, sanctuaries, and attracting songbirds and waterfowl.

The Golden Plover and Other Birds, by Arthur A. Allen. 324 pages; photographs, color plates. Cornell. Ithaca, N. Y. 1939. Out of print. These biographies of birds are beautifully told as if by the different birds themselves. The author is one of the finest ornithologists in the country, so the text is reliable and delightful at the same time. Beautiful illustrations.

Birds of the World: Their Life and Habits, by Paul Barruel. 204 pages; drawings, photographs, color plates. $12.50. Oxford. New York. 1955. A book to answer all your questions about the behavior of birds both at home and in distant lands.

Natural History of American Birds of Eastern and Central North America, by Edward H. Forbush. 553 pages; color plates. $7.50. Houghton Mifflin. Boston. 1939 (revised and abridged edition). Valuable not only for its wealth of information but for its delightful text accompanying each species of bird.

A Guide to Bird Watching, by Joseph J. Hickey. 262 pages; drawings. $4.75. Oxford. New York. 1943. Tells how to begin bird study, how to count numbers of birds in a flock or in flight, how to band birds, how birds migrate, and what to watch for when bird watching. Contains a list of bird clubs in Canada and the United States.

The Audubon Guide to Attracting Birds, edited by John H. Baker. 268 pages; photographs, diagrams, color plates. Doubleday. New York. 1941. Out of print. A group of experts tell you how to feed birds, build birdhouses, create small or large sanctuaries for both song and water birds, how to photograph and band birds, what to plant to attract birds, and how to keep bird pests like starlings and house sparrows away from your grounds.

HOW TO IDENTIFY BIRDS

A Field Guide to the Birds, by Roger Tory Peterson. 180 pages; drawings, color plates. $2.75. Houghton Mifflin. Boston. 1939 (revised edition). Covers the states east of the Rockies and of the Rio Grande valley.

A Field Guide to Western Birds, by Roger Tory Peterson. 240 pages; drawings, color plates.

$3.75. Houghton Mifflin. Boston. 1941. This is the companion volume to the one mentioned above, and deals with birds found from the Rockies and the Rio Grande valley westward.

Birds of Canada, by P. A. Taverner. 445 pages; color plates, black-and-white figures. Mc-Kay. Philadelphia. 1938. Out of print.

BIRD BANDING

Manual for Bird Banders, by Frederick C. Lincoln and Prentiss Baldwin. 112 pages; illustrations. Miscellaneous Publication 58, U. S. Department of Agriculture. Washington. 1929.

BIRD FLIGHT

Bird Flight, by Gordon Aymar. 234 pages; photographs. Dodd, Mead. New York. 1935. Out of print.

The Flight of Birds, by John H. Storer. 112 pages; photographs. $2. Cranbrook Institute. Bloomfield Hills, Mich. 1948.

Wings: of Insects, Birds and Men, by Blanche Stillson. 299 pages; drawings. $3.50. Bobbs-Merrill. Indianapolis. 1954.

INJURED BIRDS AND WILD BIRDS AS PETS

The Book of Wild Pets, by Clifford B. Moore. 553 pages; photographs. $5. Putnam. New York. 1937.

"Unusual Bird Guests," by Gertrude Viles Grover. *Audubon Magazine.* Jan., 1954, page 34 *et seq.* About sick, orphaned, and injured birds found in a garden.

"Homer the Sixth Grade Grackel," by Elizabeth Barnhill Clarkson. *Audubon Magazine.* Sept., 1948, pages 284–285.

MIGRATION

*Traveling with the Birds, by Rudyerd Boulton. $2.50. Donohue. Chicago. 1933.

The Migration of American Birds, by Frederick C. Lincoln. 189 pages; color plates, maps. Doubleday. New York. 1939. Out of print.

The Migrations of Birds, by Alexander Wetmore. 229 pages; figures, maps. Harvard. Cam-

bridge, Mass. 1930. Out of print.

"Perils of the Flyway," by Robert S. Lemmon. *Audubon Magazine.* March, 1952, page 100.

"Wings Across the Moon," by Robert J. Newman. *Audubon Magazine.* July, 1952, pages 212–218.

"The Mystery of Migration," by Ivan T. Sanderson. *Saturday Evening Post.* July 15, 1944, pages 12–13 *et seq.*

"Ten Billion Birds on the Wing," by George Dock, Jr. *Reader's Digest.* June, 1951, pages 101–104.

"Mystery of Pathfinding" (in animals, insects, fish, etc.), by Alan Devoe. *Reader's Digest.* May, 1954, pages 61–64.

NESTS

Birds' Nests: A Field Guide, by Birger Richard Headstrom. 128 pages; photographs. $3. Ives Washburn. New York. 1949. Covers the subject in the eastern states.

Birds' Nests of the West, by Birger Richard Headstrom. 177 pages; photographs. $3. Ives Washburn. New York. 1951. A companion volume to the above, for the western states.

PRIMARILY PICTURE BOOKS

The Birds of America, by John James Audubon, with foreword and descriptive captions by William Vogt. 435 pages; color plates. $8.95. Macmillan. New York. 1953 (revised edition). All the bird paintings of the immortal Audubon's original edition.

Land Birds of America, by Robert Cushman Murphy and Dean Amadon. 240 pages; color photography. $5.95. McGraw-Hill. New York. 1953.

Stalking Birds with a Color Camera, by Arthur A. Allen. 328 pages; black-and-white and color photography. $7.50. National Geographic Society. Washington. 1951.

The National Geographic Magazine has for many years been publishing bird portraits by famous painters, accompanied by informative text. Though some of these have appeared in book form later, the pictures are much fresher in the original issues of the magazine, which can be picked up inexpensively in secondhand stores. Notable are the following articles:

"Auks and Their Northland Neighbors," Jan., 1936.

"Birds of the High Seas," Aug., 1938.

"Birds of the Northern Seas," Jan., 1936.

"Birds That Cruise the Coast and Inland Waters," March, 1934.

"The Solemn, Sociable Puffins," Sept., 1954.

"Wings over the Bounding Main," Aug., 1938.

"New Guinea's Paradise of Birds," Nov., 1951.

"Strange Courtship of Birds of Paradise," Feb., 1950.

"Parrots, Kingfishers, and Flycatchers," June, 1936.

"Eagle, King of Birds, and His Kin," July, 1933.

"Shadowy Birds of the Night," Feb., 1935.

"Silent-winged Owls of North America," Feb., 1935.

"Shore Birds, Cranes, and Rails," Aug., 1937.

"Large Wading Birds" (ibises, herons, flamingos), Oct., 1932.

"The Pink Birds of Texas" (spoonbills), Nov., 1949.

"Far-Flying Wild Fowl and Their Foes," Oct., 1934.

"Game Birds of Prairie, Forest, and Tundra," Oct., 1936.

"Crows, Magpies, and Jays," Jan., 1933.

"Woodpeckers, Friends of Our Forests," April, 1933.

"Seeking the Smallest Feathered Creatures" (hummingbirds, swifts, and goatsuckers), July, 1932.

"Hummingbirds in Action," Aug., 1947.

"Blithe Birds of Dooryard, Bush, and Brake," May, 1934.

"Blackbirds and Orioles," July, 1934.

"Friends of Our Forests" (warblers), April, 1917.

"Winged Denizens of Woodland, Stream, and Marsh," May, 1934.

"Thrushes, Thrashers, and Swallows," April, 1936.

"Tanagers and Finches," April, 1935.

"Sparrows, Towhees, and Longspurs," March, 1939.

SANCTUARIES

Small Refuges for Waterfowl. 64 pages; illustrations. 25 cents. More Game Birds in America, Inc. New York. 1939 (3rd revised edition).

Song-bird Sanctuaries, by Roger Tory Peterson. Circular 19, National Audubon Society. New York. 1937.

Local Bird Refuges, by W. L. McAtee. 14 pages; illustrations. Farmers' Bulletin No. 1644. U. S. Department of Agriculture. Washington, D. C. 1931.

"Saving Man's Wildlife Heritage," by John H. Baker. *National Geographic.* Nov., 1954, pages 581–620.

"Malheur Bird Refuge" (this Oregon sanctuary is the home of a million water birds), by Grace V. Sharritt. *Natural History.* Nov., 1948, pages 400–402.

"Stream-side Sanctuaries," by Len Hofmann. *Audubon Magazine.* July, 1943, pages 194–202.

BIRTH, CHILDHOOD, AND PARENTAL CARE OF ANIMALS

The Childhood of Animals, by P. Chalmers Mitchell. 269 pages; drawings, color plates. Stokes. New York. 1912. Out of print.

"Nature's Births and Babies," by Raymond L. Ditmars. *Natural History.* Sept., 1939, pages 71–73.

"Animal Babies," by John Eric Hill. *Natural History*. May, 1944, page 213.

"Animal Baby Carriages," by John Eric Hill. *Natural History*. May, 1945, page 198.

CAMOUFLAGE IN NATURE

"Natural Camouflage." *Life*. August 6, 1951, pages 44–50.

"A Camouflage Artist Among Caterpillars," by C. H. Curran. *Natural History*. Oct., 1945, pages 360–363.

"A Desert Walking Stick" (now you see it, now you don't—as Nature defies the sharpest eye), by Lewis Wayne Walker. *Natural History*. March, 1951, pages 132–133.

"Beachcombers" (the snowy plover is a distinguished camouflage artist and a born master of diversion strategy), by Lewis Wayne Walker. *Natural History*. May, 1949, pages 232–233.

"Natural Camouflage Aids Game Birds" (how Nature protects the hunted), by Ben East. *Natural History*. Oct., 1947, pages 350–351.

"Camouflage in Nature" (strange examples in the art of concealment), by Lorus J. and Margery J. Milne. *Natural History*. April, 1950, pages 156–163.

CAREERS AND HOBBIES IN NATURE

The Book of Nature Hobbies, by Ted Pettit. 280 pages; illustrations. Didier. New York. 1947. Out of print.

Byways to Adventure: A Guide to Nature Hobbies, by Edwin Way Teale. 222 pages; photographs. Dodd, Mead. New York. 1942. Out of print.

Careers and Opportunities in Science, by Philip Pollack. 252 pages; photographs. $3.75. Dutton. New York. 1954 (revised edition).

How to Make a Home Nature Museum, by Vinson Brown. 214 pages; drawings. $2.75. Little, Brown. Boston. 1954.

Field Book of Nature Activities, by William Hillcourt. 320 pages; drawings. $3.95. Putnam. New York. 1950.

"Natural History for Everybody," by Donald Culross Peattie. *Natural History*. Feb., 1938, pages 103–107.

"Your Nature Hobby," by Donald Culross Peattie. *Natural History*. Feb., 1939, pages 69–72.

"Careers in Nature," by Donald Culross Peattie. *Natural History*. Oct., 1938, pages 165–168.

CURIOSITIES, WONDERS, AND CHAMPIONS OF THE ANIMAL WORLD

Animal Wonder World, by Frank W. Lane. 310 pages; illustrations. $4. Sheridan House. New York. 1952.

Strangest Creatures on Earth, edited by Edward M. Weyer. 255 pages; photographs. $4. Sheridan House. New York. 1953.

This Fascinating Animal World, by Alan Devoe. 303 pages; illustrations. $3.75. McGraw-Hill. New York. 1951.

Nature Is Stranger than Fiction, by John Y. Beaty. 286 pages; drawings. $2.50. Lippincott. Philadelphia. 1941. Although the title may sound like "believe it or not," the facts are solid.

Curious Creatures, by Erna Pinner. 256 pages; drawings. Philosophical Library. New York. 1954. Out of print.

"Nature's Utmosts," by Alan Devoe. *Nature Magazine*. Feb., 1950, pages 64–67. Tells about some incredible attributes with which nature has endowed her creatures: size, speed, tongues, coloration.

"Which Are the Biggest?" (an astonishing parade of Nature's record-breakers), by Osmond P. Breland. *Natural History*. Feb., 1953, pages 66–71 *et seq.*

ENCYCLOPEDIAS OF NATURE STUDY AND GENERAL GUIDES

Parade of the Animal Kingdom, by Robert Hegner. 675 pages; photographs. $5. Macmillan. New York. 1944.

The Amateur Naturalist's Handbook, by Vinson Brown. 475 pages; drawings. $3.50. Little, Brown. Boston. 1948.

Fieldbook of Natural History, by E. Laurence Palmer. 664 pages; illustrations. $8. McGraw-Hill. New York. 1949.

The Animal Kingdom, edited by Frederick Drimmer. 3 volumes; drawings, photographs, color plates. $17.50. Greystone. New York. 1954.

FISHES

GENERAL BOOKS

The Wonder World of Fishes, by Ida M. Mellen. 160 pages; illustrations. $3. Dodd, Mead. New York. 1951.

The Ways of Fishes, by Leonard P. Schultz, with Edith M. Stern. 264 pages; illustrations, maps. $5. Van Nostrand. New York. 1948.

The Book of Fishes, edited by John Oliver La Gorce. 339 pages, color and monochrome illustrations. $6.50. National Geographic Society. Washington, D. C. 1952 (revised and enlarged edition).

FRESH-WATER FISHES

Fishes of the Great Lakes Region, by Carl L. Hubbs and Karl F. Lagler. 186 pages; photographs, drawings, color plates, diagrams, maps. $3. Bulletin 26. Cranbrook Institute. Bloomfield Hills, Mich. 1948.

Field Book of Fresh-water Fishes of North America, by Ray Schrenkeisen. 312 pages; illustrations. Putnam. New York. 1938. Out of print.

MARINE FISHES

Marine Fishes of the Atlantic Coast, by Charles M. Breder, Jr. 375 pages; drawings, color plates. $5. Putnam. New York. 1940.

MIGRATION OF FISHES

Fishes: Their Journeys and Migrations, by Louis Roule. 270 pages; illustrations. Norton. New York. 1933. Out of print.

"The Story of the Fish Anguilla" (the solution of the mystery of how eels reproduce their kind), by Willy Ley. *Natural History*. Feb., 1949, pages 82–85 *et seq.*

"The Itinerant Eel" (rendezvous with life in the Sargasso: the beginning of the eel's migration), by Paul Bulla. *Natural History*. May, 1942, pages 257–259.

TROPICAL FISH

"Warm-Sea Fishes" (paintings in color). *National Geographic*. Jan., 1921, pages 61–69.

"Treasure-house of the Gulf Stream," by John Oliver La Gorce. *National Geographic*. Jan., 1921, pages 53–68.

"Interesting Citizens of the Gulf Stream," by John T. Nichols. *National Geographic*. Jan., 1921, pages 69–84.

"Tropical Toy Fishes," by Ida Mellen. *National Geographic*. March, 1931, pages 286–317.

"Iridescent Denizens of the Miniature Aquarium" (paintings in color). *National Geographic*. March, 1931, pages 291–300.

"Life on a Coral Reef," by W. H. Longley. *National Geographic*. Jan., 1927.

FROGS, TOADS, NEWTS, AND SALAMANDERS (AMPHIBIANS)

Amphibians and Reptiles of Western North America, by Robert C. Stebbins. 528 pages; drawings, maps. $8.50. McGraw-Hill. New York. 1954.

The Frog Book, by Mary C. Dickerson. 253 pages; drawings, color plates. Doubleday. New York. 1937. Out of print.

Handbook of Frogs and Toads of the United States and Canada, by Albert Hazen Wright and Anna Allen Wright. 640 pages; color plates, photographs, maps. $6.50. Cornell. Ithaca, N. Y. 1949 (3rd edition).

Handbook of Salamanders, by S. C. Bishop. 555 pages; photographs, drawings, maps. $6. Cornell. Ithaca, N. Y. 1943.

INSECTS AND SPIDERS

GENERAL BOOKS AND ARTICLES

Grassroot Jungles, by Edwin Way Teale. 240 pages; photographs. $5. Dodd, Mead. New York. 1944 (revised and enlarged edition).

Near Horizons, the story of an insect garden, by Edwin Way Teale. 319 pages; photographs. Dodd, Mead. New York. 1942. Out of print.

Insect Adventures, retold from Alexander Teixeira de Mattos' translation of Fabre's *Souvenirs Entomologiques,* by Louise Seymour Hasbrouck. 287 pages; illustrations. $2.75. Dodd, Mead. New York. 1950.

Little Lives, by Julie Closson Kenly. 271 pages; drawings. Appleton-Century. New York. 1938. Out of print.

Voices from the Grass, by Julie Closson Kenly. 248 pages; drawings. Appleton-Century. New York. 1940. Out of print.

The Fabulous Insects, edited by Charles Neider. 278 pages. $3.50. Harper. New York. 1954. A collection of exciting nature stories about insect life.

The Book of Insect Oddities, by Raymond L. Ditmars. 62 pages; drawings, color plates. Lippincott. Philadelphia. 1938. Out of print.

Insects: Their Secret World, by Evelyn Cheesman. 246 pages; drawings. $3.50. Sloane. New York. 1953.

Animal Sounds, by George F. Mason. 96 pages; drawings. $2.25. Morrow. New York. 1948.

"In Praise of Insects," by Herbert F. Schwarz. *Audubon Magazine.* March, 1945, pages 90–100.

HOW TO IDENTIFY INSECTS

Boys' Book of Insects, by Edwin Way Teale. 237 pages; drawings, photographs. Dutton. New York. 1939. Out of print.

The Insect Guide, orders and major families of North American insects, by Ralph B. Swain. 261 pages; drawings, color plates. $3.95. Doubleday. New York. 1948.

Field Book of Insects (of the United States and Canada, aiming to answer common questions), by Frank E. Lutz. 510 pages; drawings, color plates. $4.50. Putnam. New York. 1935 (3rd revised edition).

ANTS

The Life of the Ant, by Maurice Maeterlinck. 282 pages. Day. New York. 1930. Out of print.

The Ways of the Ant, by John Crompton. 242 pages; drawings. $3.50. Houghton Mifflin. Boston. 1954.

"The Ants' Camels" (the ant domesticates many more kinds of animals than man does), by Edwin Way Teale. *Natural History.* Dec., 1948, pages 456–461.

"Consider the Harvester Ant" (it harvests grain

like any provident farmer and after wet weather dries it on the roof in the sun), by Ross E. Hutchins. *Natural History.* June, 1953, pages 256–259.

"Stalking Ants, Savage and Civilized," by William M. Mann. *National Geographic.* Aug., 1934, pages 171–192.

"Work and War in the World of Ants" (paintings in color). *National Geographic.* Aug., 1934, pages 179–186.

"Living Casks of Honey," by Jennie E. Harris. *National Geographic.* Aug., 1934, pages 193–199.

"Toilers That Live Underfoot" (a photographic record of everyday life among the ants). *Life.* Dec. 6, 1954, pages 169–173.

BEES

The Life of the Bee, by Maurice Maeterlinck. 427 pages. $3. Dodd, Mead. New York. 1930.

Bees' Ways, by George De Clyver Curtis. 240 pages. $2.75. Houghton Mifflin. Boston. 1948.

The Golden Throng: A Book About Bees, by Edwin Way Teale. 208 pages; photographs. Dodd, Mead. New York. 1940. Out of print.

Bees: Their Vision, Chemical Senses, and Language, by Karl von Frisch. 119 pages; illustrations. Cornell. Ithaca, N. Y. 1950. Out of print.

"Charade of the Honeybee" (a breath-taking discovery reveals how a bee can "draw a flight map" and tell its hivemates where to find honey), by N. J. Berrill. *Natural History.* Feb., 1951, pages 68–71.

"Man's Winged Ally, the Busy Honeybee," by James I. Hambleton. *National Geographic.* April, 1935, pages 401–428.

BEETLES

"Nature's Undertaker" (fantastic sexton beetle sees to the burial of many small animals), by Alan Devoe. *Reader's Digest.* Feb., 1951, pages 13–14.

BUTTERFLIES AND MOTHS

Field Guide to the Butterflies of North America, East of the Great Plains, by Alexander B. Klots. 349 pages; drawings, photographs, color plates. $3.75. Houghton Mifflin. Boston. 1951.

The Butterfly Book, a popular guide to a knowledge of the butterflies of North America, by W. J. Holland. 424 pages; drawings, color plates. $12.50. Doubleday. New York. 1940 (revised and enlarged edition).

Butterflies, a handbook of the butterflies of the United States, complete for the region north of the Potomac and Ohio rivers and east of the Dakotas, by Ralph Macy and Harold H. Shepard. 247 pages; photographs, color plates, maps. University of Minnesota. Minneapolis. 1941. Out of print.

"Butterflies, Try and Get Them," by Laurence Ilsley Hewes. *National Geographic.* May, 1936, pages 666–678.

"Butterfly Farm," by Dée Bredin. *Reader's Digest.* March, 1948, page 136.

"Strange Habits of Familiar Moths and Butterflies," by William Joseph Showalter. *National Geographic.* July, 1927, pages 76–126.

"Marked Monarchs" (tracing the migration of the monarch butterfly), by F. A. Urquhart. *Natural History.* May, 1952, pages 226–228.

"Butterfly Travelers," by C. B. Williams. *National Geographic.* May, 1937, pages 568–585.

CICADAS

"Mr. Big Noise" (the 17-year cicada), by Donald Culross Peattie. *Reader's Digest.* May, 1951, pages 94–97.

DRAGONFLIES

"The Dragonfly, Terror of the Insect World," by Alan Devoe. *Reader's Digest.* Dec., 1946, pages 63–64.

"The Two Lives of Anax" (the life cycle of a green darner), by Roy L. Abbott. *Natural History.* May, 1946, pages 204–208.

GRASSHOPPERS AND LOCUSTS

The Grasshopper Book, by Wilfrid S. Bronson. 127 pages; diagrams, drawings. $2.75. Harcourt, Brace. New York. 1943.

"War on the Locust" (unified international efforts from West Africa to India are making progress against an insect that has plagued man since Biblical times), by B. P. Uvarov. *Natural History.* Dec., 1953, pages 446–449.

"Year of the Locust," by Edwin Muller. *Reader's Digest.* July, 1953, pages 58–60.

MANTISES

"Praying Mantis" (photographs). *National Geographic.* May, 1950, pages 685–692.

"The Story of the Praying Mantis" (a photoserial in three acts). *Natural History.* June, 1939, pages 38–40.

SPIDERS

American Spiders, by Willis J. Gertsch. 285 pages; photographs, diagrams, color plates. $7.50. Van Nostrand. New York. 1949.

The Spider Book, by John Henry Comstock. 729 pages; drawings, photographs. $6. Cornell. Ithaca, N. Y. 1948.

Black Widow: America's Most Poisonous Spider, by Raymond W. Thorp and Weldon D. Woodson. 256 pages; photographs. $3. University of North Carolina. Chapel Hill. 1945. Definitely scary!

"California Trapdoor Spider Performs Engineering Marvels," by Lee Passmore. *National Geographic.* Aug., 1933, pages 195–211.

"Nature's Ingenious Spinners" (paintings in color). *National Geographic.* Aug., 1933, pages 167–174.

"The Jumping Spider," by Walker Van Riper. *Natural History.* Dec., 1945, page 467.

"Spider Silk, Wonder-stuff of Nature," by Donald Culross Peattie. *Nature Magazine.* June, 1945, pages 289–292 *et seq.*

"The Funnel-web Spider" (a picture story), by Lee Passmore. *Natural History.* Feb., 1940, pages 80–83.

WASPS

"Farmers' Friends Among the Wasps and Hornets" (paintings in color). *National Geographic.* July, 1937, pages 57–64.

"Potent Personalities, Wasps and Hornets," by Austin H. Clark. *National Geographic.* July, 1937, pages 47–72.

LIGHT IN ANIMAL LIFE

"Living Lamps," by N. J. Berrill. *Natural History.* Jan., 1949, pages 36–41.

"Miracle of the Firefly," by Donald Culross Peattie. *Reader's Digest.* Nov., 1949, pages 86–88.

"Flashes from Ocean Deeps" (paintings in color). *National Geographic.* Dec., 1934, pages 677–700.

"Luminous Life in the Depths of the Sea" (paintings in color). *National Geographic.* June, 1931, pages 667–674.

For further details about luminous animals of the ocean, see SEA AND SHORE LIFE, *page* 315.

LOCALITIES OF SPECIAL INTEREST

Gulf Coast Adventure, by Sam and Bess Woolford and Fritz and Emilie Toepperwein. $2. Highland Press. Boerne, Texas. 1953.

Desert Parade: A Guide to Southwestern Desert Plants and Wildlife, by William Carr. 96 pages; photographs, maps. Viking. New York. 1947. Out of print.

"The World We Live In: Part X: The Arctic Barrens," by Lincoln Barnett. *Life.* June 7, 1954, pages 90–109 *et seq.*

"The World We Live In: Part XI: The Rain Forest," by Lincoln Barnett. *Life.* Sept. 20, 1954, pages 76–99 *et seq.*

"The World We Live In: Part XII: The Woods

of Home," by Lincoln Barnett. *Life*. Nov. 8, 1954, pages 78–97 *et seq*.

"Big Bend National Park," by Sidney Ross. *Natural History*. May, 1949, pages 216–220.

"The Wonderland of the Florida Keys," by Robert P. Allen. *Audubon Magazine*. Nov., 1946, pages 342–347.

"In the Realm of the Spanish Moss" (from Gulf Coast of Texas through Florida and up the Atlantic Coast to Virginia), by Gladys M. Relyea. *Audubon Magazine*. Nov., 1950, pages 362–369.

LOCOMOTION OF ANIMALS (EXCEPT FLIGHT)

How Animals Move, by James Gray. 114 pages; photographs, drawings. $3. Cambridge. New York. 1953.

"Design for Swimming" (many of man's inventions were discovered by fishes ages ago), by G. Miles Conrad. *Natural History*. Oct., 1942, pages 140–146.

"Tree-climbing Snakes" (seemingly impossible feats are performed by certain snakes), by C. M. Bogert. *Natural History*. June, 1953, pages 281–283.

"Flying Squirrels, Nature's Gliders," by Ernest P. Walker. *National Geographic*. May, 1947, pages 662–674.

For flight, see that subject under BIRDS, *page 303*.

MAMMALS

GENERAL BOOKS

Animals on the March, by W. Maxwell Reed and Janette M. Lucas. 335 pages; photographs (mostly of museum exhibition cases and specimens), maps of the world (in other geologic ages). Harcourt, Brace. New York. 1937. Out of print. An excellent book, dealing mostly with the evolution of our most common animals through geologic ages to the present.

A Child's Story of the Animal World, by Edward G. Huey. 355 pages; photographs, drawings. Reynal & Hitchcock. New York. 1935. Out of print.

Homes and Habits of Wild Animals, by Karl Patterson Schmidt. 64 pages; drawings, color plates. $2.50. Donohue. Chicago. 1934.

Animals in American History: A Picture Book, by Paul Bransom, with text by Helen Dean Fish. 50 pages; drawings. Stokes. New York. 1939. Out of print.

Mammals of North America, by Victor H. Cahalane. 682 pages; drawings. $5.95. Macmillan. New York. 1947. This is the finest all-round book on American mammals.

Animals of the World, edited by J. Walker McSpadden. 354 pages; photographs and paintings in color. Doubleday. New York. 1942. Out of print.

Speaking of Animals, by Alan Devoe. 198 pages; photographs. Creative Age. New York. 1948. Out of print. Popularly written accounts of some mammals and a few other creatures.

Lives of Game Animals, by Ernest Thompson Seton. 8 volumes; drawings, maps. $50. Branford. Boston. 1953. The most complete study ever made not only of "game" animals but of almost all North American mammals except bats and seagoing sorts. A magnificent work, delightfully illustrated, and in a scientific class far above this author's unreliable animal fiction. Though not especially written for young readers, they will find it easy going.

Wild Animals of the World, by William Bridges and Mary Baker. 272 pages; color plates. $3.95. Doubleday. New York. 1948.

Audubon's Animals, compiled and edited by Alice Ford. 222 pages; drawings, color plates. Crowell. New York. 1951. Out of print. Audubon's illustrations of *The Quad-*

rupeds of North America, with brief selections from the text.

HOW TO IDENTIFY MAMMALS

Field Book of North American Mammals, by H. E. Anthony. 674 pages; drawings, color plates, charts. $6. Putnam. New York. 1928.

The Mammal Guide, mammals of North America, north of Mexico, by Ralph S. Palmer. 384 pages; color plates, drawings, maps. $4.95. Doubleday. New York. 1954.

A Field Guide to the Mammals, by W. H. Burt and R. P. Grossenheider. 200 pages; color plates, black-and-white plates, maps. $3.75. Houghton Mifflin. Boston. 1952.

"The Larger North American Mammals," by Edward W. Nelson. *National Geographic.* Nov., 1916, pages 385–472.

"Smaller Mammals of North America," by Edward W. Nelson. *National Geographic.* May, 1918, pages 371–493.

BATS

"Our Flying Mammals of the Night," by Hartley H. T. Jackson. *Audubon Magazine.* March, 1953, pages 74–77.

"Tenants of the House," by Josephine Johnson. *Atlantic Monthly.* Aug., 1952, pages 39–42.

"Portrait of a Vampire," by Joseph Bernstein. *Natural History.* Feb., 1952, pages 82–87 *et seq.*

"Mystery Mammals of the Twilight," by Donald R. Griffin. *National Geographic.* July, 1946, pages 117–134.

BEAVERS

"The Return of the Fur Brigade" (how Colorado's threatened beaver population was restored), by Arthur H. Carhart. *Natural History.* Feb., 1944, pages 68–71.

"Beaver Show" (700 nights in the front row), by Edwin Way Teale. *Natural History.* Nov., 1944, pages 390–395.

"Signs of Beaver" (nature's master engineer and flood control expert), by T. Donald Carter. *Natural History.* April, 1953, pages 160–161.

"Beaver Engineers" (beavers accomplish difficult engineering feats and leave a fertile meadow behind), by John Eric Hill. *Natural History.* June, 1943, pages 41–43.

BISON OR BUFFALO

The American Bison, by Martin S. Garretson. 244 pages; photographs. $1.10. New York Zoological Society. New York. 1938.

"America's Greatest Host" (the story of Old Man Buffalo and his role in American history), by Donald Culross Peattie. *Natural History.* Oct., 1943, pages 112–114.

DEER FAMILY: ANTELOPE, CARIBOU, DEER, ELK, AND MOOSE

People of the Deer, by Farley Mowat. 344 pages; drawings, maps. $5. Little, Brown. Boston. 1952. A very fine true story of life in the Canadian Far North.

"Deer of the World," by Victor H. Cahalane. *National Geographic.* Oct., 1939, pages 463–510.

"In Caribou Land," by Francis Harper. *Natural History.* May, 1949, pages 224–231 *et seq.*

"Where the Antelope Play," by William H. Carr. *Natural History.* June, 1947, pages 276–281.

DOG FAMILY: WILD DOGS, COYOTES, FOXES, AND WOLVES

The Voice of the Coyote, by J. Frank Dobie. 386 pages; drawings. $5. Little, Brown. Boston. 1949. A wonderful book on the life and lore of this "sly dog."

"Coyote Cunning," by Lewis Nordyke. *Nature Magazine.* March, 1944, pages 120–124.

"Wonder Dog" (defense of the coyote), by Olaus J. Murie. *Audubon Magazine.* Sept., 1948, pages 268–275.

"The Smart Coyote" (truly he lives by his wits), by J. Frank Dobie. *Natural History.* Feb., 1942, pages 70–75.

DOMESTICATION OF ANIMALS

"The Domestication of Animals," by Clark Wissler. *Natural History*. May, 1945, pages 200–206.

"Where the Cats Came From," by Edwin H. Colbert (comp.). *Natural History*. Dec., 1940, pages 288–289.

"The Taurine World," by Alvin Howard Sanders. *National Geographic*. Dec., 1925, pages 591–710.

"The Cattle of the World" (paintings in color). *National Geographic*. Dec., 1925, pages 639–678.

"Wild Dogs and Tame, Past and Present" (a panorama of the origin, genealogy, and "social" background of the tractable wolf that emerged from the wilderness to become man's best friend), by Edwin H. Colbert. *Natural History*. Feb., 1939, pages 90–101.

"Arctic Nomads" (a glimpse into the life of the Lapps), by Irene Morden. *Natural History*. Jan., 1952, pages 24–29. Concerns reindeer.

SEAGOING MAMMALS: SEALS, SEA LIONS, SEA OTTERS, WHALES, ETC.

A Seal's World, an account of the first three years in the life of a harp seal, by Frank Stuart. 223 pages; decorations, map. McGraw-Hill. New York. 1954. Out of print.

The Hunting of the Silver Fleece, by Fredericka Martin. 328 pages; photographs. Greenberg. New York. 1946. Out of print.

"Sea Lions," by Mark Huling. *Reader's Digest*. Dec., 1944, pages 70–72.

"Winning Ways of the Sea Otter," by Alan Devoe. *Reader's Digest*. June, 1944, pages 29–31.

"Return of the Sea Elephant" (one of the most curious mammals of the sea shows signs of coming back), by Lewis Wayne Walker. *Natural History*. Nov., 1947, pages 408–411.

"Parky" (the story of a baby walrus that traveled south), by Woodbridge Williams. *Natural History*. Jan., 1941, pages 40–45.

"Sea Giant at Play" (whales), by Alfred C. Glassel, Jr. *Natural History*. Feb., 1953, pages 63–66.

"Whales, Giants of the Sea," by Remington Kellogg. *National Geographic*. Jan., 1940, pages 35–90.

SHEEP AND GOATS (WILD)

"Arizona Sheep Trek," by Francis R. Line. *National Geographic*. April, 1950, pages 457–478.

"Bighorns on the Border," by Arthur F. Halloran. *Audubon Magazine*. Nov., 1947, pages 332–337.

"The Mountain Goat" (hardy inhabitant of the Rockies), by Osmond P. Breland. *Audubon Magazine*. May, 1954, pages 112–113.

WILD MAMMALS AS PETS

Our Small Native Mammals: Their Habits and Care, by Robert Snedigar. 308 pages; illustrations. Random House. New York. 1939. Out of print. Tells how to start a home zoo.

The Book of Wild Pets, by Clifford B. Moore. 553 pages; photographs. $5. Putnam. New York. 1937.

WOODCHUCKS

"Your Neighbor the Woodchuck," by Dave Cook. *Audubon Magazine*. July, 1945, pages 201–206.

"Exploring the World of 'Whistle Pig'" (woodchuck), by W. J. Hamilton. *Audubon Magazine*. March, 1950, pages 96–101.

"Biography of a Whistlepig," by Roy L. Abbott. *Natural History*. Feb., 1939, pages 112–116.

NIGHT AND ANIMAL LIFE

Eyes in the Night, by Tappan Gregory. 243 pages; photographs. Crowell. New York. 1939. Out of print.

"Exploring the Night" (while man escapes the dark in sleep or by artificial light, a host of creatures enact their dramas in the brooding corridors of night), by Lorus J. and Margery J. Milne. *Natural History.* Oct., 1953, pages 344–351.

"Shadowy Birds of the Night" (owls), by Alexander Wetmore. *National Geographic.* Feb.,

1935, pages 217–240.

"Voices of the Night" (toads and frogs), by Arthur A. Allen. *National Geographic.* April, 1950, pages 507–522.

PLANTS

GENERAL BOOKS

The World of Plant Life, by Clarence J. Hylander. 653 pages; photographs, drawings. $8.95. Macmillan. New York. 1956 (2nd edition). This, though not designed for young readers, will answer most of their questions about plant life. A treasure chest of information and illustration.

This Green World, by Rutherford Platt. 222 pages; drawings, photographs, color plates. $6. Dodd, Mead. New York. 1942.

Flowering Earth, by Donald Culross Peattie. 260 pages; wood engravings. $3.75. Putnam. New York. 1939.

TREES

Knowing Your Trees, by G. H. Collingwood and Warren D. Brush. 328 pages; photographs, maps. $6. American Forestry Association. Washington, D. C. 1955 (new and revised edition). Each printing has been an enlargement of the previous one. Many of the maps are most unreliable, but the photographs are extensive and detailed.

Trees of the Eastern United States and Canada, by William M. Harlow. 288 pages; photographs, color plates. McGraw-Hill. New York. 1942. Out of print.

A Natural History of Trees of Eastern and Central North America, by Donald Culross Peattie. 606 pages; drawings, maps. $5. Houghton Mifflin. Boston. 1950. Besides telling how to identify trees this book contains material on American history, historic trees, the uses of trees by Indians and by the pioneers.

A Natural History of Western Trees, by Donald Culross Peattie. 751 pages; drawings, maps.

$6. Houghton Mifflin. Boston. 1953. A companion volume to the one above.

Guide to Southern Trees, by Elwood S. and J. George Harrar. 712 pages; drawings. $6. McGraw-Hill. New York. 1946.

Rocky Mountain Trees, by Richard J. Preston. 285 pages; drawings, maps. Iowa State College. Ames. 1947 (2nd edition). Out of print.

Big Trees of the Giant Forest, by George W. Stewart. 105 pages; photographs. Robertson. San Francisco. 1930. Out of print.

"Avenue of the Giants" (coast redwoods), by Donald Culross Peattie. *Holiday.* March, 1954, pages 58–63 *et seq.*

"The Mystery of the Twisted Trees" (do they reflect the spin of the earth or the effect of strictly local influences?), by Paul M. Sears. *Natural History.* Dec., 1950, pages 468–473.

"Among the Big Trees of California," by John R. White. *National Geographic.* Aug., 1934, pages 218–232.

"California's Coastal Redwood Realm," by J. R. Hildebrand. *National Geographic.* Feb., 1939, pages 133–184.

WILD FLOWERS

The Macmillan Wild Flower Book, by Clarence J. Hylander. 480 pages; color plates. $15. Macmillan. New York. 1954.

American Wild Flowers, by Harold N. Moldenke. 453 pages; photographs, color plates. $6.95. Van Nostrand. New York. 1949.

Field Book of American Wild Flowers, by F. Schuyler Mathews. 601 pages; drawings, color plates. $5. Putnam. New York. 1955 (revised and enlarged edition). Valuable chiefly in New England. The illustrations are of high quality.

The Illustrated Encyclopedia of American Wild Flowers, by Ethel Hausman. 534 pages; drawings, color plates. Doubleday. New York. 1947. Out of print.

Wild Flower Guide: Northeastern and Midland United States, by Edgar T. Wherry. 202 pages; drawings, color plates. $3.95. Doubleday. New York. 1948.

Field Book of Western Wild Flowers, by Margaret Armstrong, in collaboration with J. J. Thornber. 644 pages; drawings, color plates. $5. Putnam. New York. 1915. Still the best book in its field, with fine illustrations, but even so it is very sketchy, only hitting high spots here and there.

Flowers of Coast and Sierra, by Edith S. Clements. 226 pages; color plates. $4.50. Wilson. New York. 1928. Though very sketchy this is still the best popular book on California wild flowers we have.

Texas Flowers in Natural Colors, by Eula Whitehouse. 212 pages; color plates. $3.95. Southern Methodist University. Dallas. 1948.

"American Wild Flowers." *National Geographic.* May, 1915, pages 483–517.

"Midsummer Wild Flowers." *National Geographic.* July, 1922, pages 35–59.

"Wild Flowers of the West," by Edith S. Clements. *National Geographic.* May, 1927, pages 564–622.

POND LIFE

*Beginner's Guide to Fresh-water Life, by L. A. Hausman. 128 pages; illustrations. $2.50. Putnam. New York. 1950.

Streams, Lakes, Ponds and the Life in Them, by R. E. Coker. 345 pages; illustrations. $6. University of North Carolina. Chapel Hill. 1954.

Field Book of Ponds and Streams (an introduc-

tion to the life of fresh water), by Ann Haven Morgan. 448 pages; drawings, photographs, color plates. $5. Putnam. New York. 1930.

"The Life of the Water Film" (water is not wet for many small animals and plants), by Lorus J. and Margery J. Milne. *Natural History.* June, 1947, pages 248–254.

REPTILES

*Boy's Book of Snakes, by Percy A. Morris. 185 pages; illustrations. $3.50. Ronald. New York. 1948.

Reptiles of the World, by Raymond L. Ditmars. 321 pages; photographs. $5.95. Macmillan. New York. 1933 (new revised edition).

The Reptile Book, by Raymond L. Ditmars. 471 pages; photographs, color plates. Doubleday. New York. 1907. Out of print.

The Reptiles of North America, by Raymond L. Ditmars. 476 pages; photographs, color plates. $7.50. Doubleday. New York. 1936 (new revised edition).

Snakes of the World, by Raymond L. Ditmars. 207 pages; photographs. $4.95. Macmillan. New York. 1931.

A Field Book of North American Snakes, by

Raymond L. Ditmars. 305 pages; photographs. $4.50. Doubleday. New York. 1945.

Amphibians and Reptiles of Western North America, by Robert C. Stebbins. 528 pages; drawings, maps. $8.50. McGraw-Hill. New York. 1954.

Handbook of Lizards, by Hobart M. Smith. 557 pages; photographs. $6. Cornell. Ithaca, N. Y. 1946.

*Animals in Armor, by Clarence J. Hylander. 203 pages; photographs. $3.50. Macmillan. New York. 1954. Concerns turtles.

Handbook of Turtles, by Archie Carr. 542 pages; illustrations, maps. $7.50. Cornell. Ithaca, N. Y. 1952.

Turtles of the United States and Canada, by

Clifford H. Pope. 343 pages; photographs. $5. Knopf. New York. 1939.

"The Beneficial Serpent" (fascinating facts about creatures that both kill and cure), by Charles M. Bogert. *Natural History.* Dec., 1943, pages 234–236.

"Are You Afraid of Snakes?" (popular prejudices and fallacies discussed), by William H. Carr. *Natural History.* May, 1945, pages 232–234.

"Adventures in Python Country" (through the Borneo jungles on the trail of the world's largest snake), by Harry C. Raven. *Natural History.* Jan., 1946, pages 38–41.

SEA AND SHORE LIFE (not including fishes, sea shells, and seagoing mammals)

*Beginner's Guide to Seashore Life, by Leon A. Hausman. 128 pages; illustrations. $2. Putnam. New York. 1949.

*Gulf Coast Adventure, by Sam and Bess Woolford and Fritz and Emilie Toepperwein. 64 pages; illustrations. $2. Highland Press. Boerne, Texas. 1953.

Field Book of Seashore Life, by Roy Waldo Miner. 630 pages; photographs, drawings, color plates. $7. Putnam. New York.

*Sea and Shore, by Clarence J. Hylander. 242 pages; illustrations. $3. Macmillan. New York. 1950.

Under the Sea-wind, by Rachel L. Carson. 314 pages; color drawings, diagrams. $4. Oxford. New York. 1952. This is a charming book about seashore life.

The Book of the Sea, edited by A. C. Spectorsky. 488 pages; drawings, photographs. $10. Appleton-Century. New York. 1954.

"The World We Live In: Part II: The Miracle of the Sea," by Lincoln Barnett. *Life.* Feb. 9, 1953, pages 58–77 *et seq.*

"Chrysanthemum of the Sea" (is it a flower that moves or an animal whose head is a blossom?), by Woody Williams. *Natural History.* Sept., 1951, pages 318–319.

"Living Jewels of the Sea" (microscopic crustaceans), by William Crowder. *National Geographic.* Sept., 1927, pages 290–304.

"Crabs and Crablike Curiosities of the Sea," by William Crowder. *National Geographic.* July, 1928, pages 56–72.

"Coral Castle Builders of Tropic Seas," by Roy Waldo Miner. *National Geographic.* June, 1934, pages 703–728.

"Multi-hued Marvels of a Coral Reef" (paintings in color). *National Geographic.* June, 1934, pages 719–726.

"Marauders of the Sea" (squid and octopuses), by Roy Waldo Miner. *National Geographic.* Aug., 1935, pages 185–207.

"Strange Creatures of Sunny Seas" (paintings in color of crabs, men-of-war, sea nettles, crayfish, snails, oysters, sponges). *National Geographic.* Feb., 1937, pages 211–218.

"The Edge of the Edge of the World" (on the brink of a submerged cliff 7,000 feet high), by Gilbert C. Klingel. *Natural History.* Feb., 1940, pages 68–73.

Half Mile Down, by William Beebe. 344 pages; photographs, color plates. $6. Duell, Sloan and Pearce. New York. 1951 (new edition).

"A Half Mile Down" (marine life from bathysphere), by William Beebe. *National Geographic.* Dec., 1934, pages 661–704.

"The Depths of the Sea," by William Beebe. *National Geographic.* Jan., 1932, pages 64–88.

SHELLS

The Shell Book, by Julia Ellen Rogers. 503 pages; photographs, color plates. $7.50. Branford. Boston. 1951 (revised edition). This old classic has been brought up to date. It is popular in style and holds its price down very well compared with other books.

Florida Sea Shells, by Bertha D. E. Aldrich and Ethel Snyder. 126 pages; photographs. $2.50. Houghton Mifflin. Boston. 1936.

A Field Guide to the Shells of Our Atlantic and Gulf Coasts, by Percy A. Morris. 236 pages; black-and-white and color photographs. $3.75. Houghton Mifflin. Boston. 1951 (revised and enlarged 2nd edition).

"What Is a Mollusk Shell?" by Roy Waldo Miner. *Natural History.* June, 1937, pages 398–409.

"In Search of the Golden Cowrie" (the objective was this rare treasure of the sea, but nightfall in Fiji brought other surprises), by R. Tucker Abbott. *Natural History.* March, 1951, pages 104–110 *et seq.*

SOUNDS AND SONGS

*Animal Sounds, by George F. Mason. 96 pages; drawings. $2.25. Morrow. New York. 1948.

"Can Music Charm Snakes?" (an account in which an amateur naturalist and a professional scientist arrive at opposite conclusions), by Bucky McDonnell. *Natural History.* Sept., 1950, pages 330–331.

"Insect Thermometers" (know the insect orchestra and you can clock the temperature), by Cleve Hallenbeck. *Natural History.* June, 1949, pages 256–259 *et seq.*

"The Kettledrum Choir of June" (the stirring love song of the bullfrogs' voices, the spirit of the marshlands), by Ben East. *Natural History.* June, 1950, pages 278–282.

SPEED OF ANIMALS

Speed in Animals, their specialization for running and leaping, by A. Brazier Howell. 270 pages; drawings. University of Chicago. Chicago. 1944. Out of print.

"Speedy Animals" (how the various four-footed creatures would show up on the race track),

by John Eric Hill. *Natural History.* Oct., 1945, page 359.

"Submarine Rockets" (some strange dramas of the deep enacted by squids, faster than any fish in the sea), by N. J. Berrill. *Natural History.* March, 1951, pages 128–132.

SPRING

"Signs of Spring," by Stanton G. Ernst. *Audubon Magazine.* March, 1943, pages 66–70.

"From Spring to Summer," by Edwin Way Teale. *Reader's Digest.* April, 1954, pages 97–101.

"First Signs of Spring" (March is heydey for Nature enthusiasts with its many advance notices of spring), by Harold K. Whitford. *Natural History.* March, 1947, pages 112–115.

"March Madness" (seasonal changes in the animal world), by John Eric Hill. *Natural History.* March, 1943, page 135.

"First Creatures of Spring" (photographs of salamanders and frogs), by Charles J. Stine. *Audubon Magazine.* March, 1954, pages 72–73.

"Spring Wild Flowers," by Donald Culross Peattie. *Holiday.* March, 1947, pages 112–116.

"Spring Song in the Trees," by Donald Culross Peattie. *Holiday.* April, 1947, pages 58–59.

"Appointment with Spring," by Donald Culross Peattie. *Holiday.* May, 1949, pages 106–107 *et seq.*

WINTER IN THE ANIMAL WORLD:
ACTIVITIES, TRACKS, HIBERNATION

A Field Guide to Animal Tracks, by Olaus Murie. 374 pages; drawings. $3.75. Houghton Mifflin. Boston. 1954.

*Animal Tracks, by George F. Mason. 95 pages; diagrams. $2.25. Morrow. New York. 1943.

Field Book of Animals in Winter, by Ann Haven Morgan. 527 pages; drawings, photographs, color plates. $5. Putnam. New York. 1939.

"How to Know Footprints" (deciphering the movements and moods of animals unseen), by Ellsworth Jaeger. *Natural History.* Nov., 1939, pages 226–232.

"Winter Roosts of Birds," by F. J. Freeman. *Audubon Magazine.* Jan., 1953, pages 33–35.

"A Time to Meet Nature," by Alan Devoe. *Audubon Magazine.* Jan., 1953, pages 6–8.

"Winter Woodsmen" (here are some of the creatures that stay to explore the magic of the winter forest), by John L. Blackford. *Natural History.* Feb., 1944, pages 72–76.

"Where Do Insects Go in Winter?" (the insects' triumph over cold), by Edwin Way Teale. *Natural History.* Jan., 1943, pages 28–37.

"The Big Sleep Is On," by Will Barker. *Natural History.* Nov., 1954, pages 402–405.

"Winter," by Donald Culross Peattie. *Holiday.* Dec., 1949, pages 114–117 *et seq.*

FILMS ABOUT NATURE

The following films are available on a rental basis from the Photo & Film Department, National Audubon Society, 1130 Fifth Avenue, New York 28, New York. All the films available from the Society are on 16 mm. reels of noninflammable safety stock. For further information about those listed and many others you can consult the Audubon "Audio-Visual Catalog," published by the Society and sold at ten cents per copy.

In addition, free catalogues of films on Nature are obtainable by writing to the Department of Films, The American Museum of Natural History, Central Park West at 79th Street, New York 24, New York, and to the Fish and Wildlife Service, U. S. Department of Interior, Box 128, College Park, Maryland.

GENERAL FILMS ABOUT BIRDS

"Audubon, the Naturalist." Script by Roger Tory Peterson. 10 min., color, sound, rental $3.50, shipping charge 50 cents. By means of oil paintings, drawings, posters, and colorful sketches, this film describes how James John Audubon devoted his life to the study of birds and animals of America.

"The Bluebird." 11 min., color, sound, rental $3.50, shipping charge 50 cents. Covers the bluebird's summer visit in the North where it competes with the wrens and starlings for nesting sites. It includes bird song, care and feeding of young, economic value, and also shows five species of woodpeckers.

"The Robin." 10 min., color, sound, rental $3.50, shipping charge 50 cents. This is an instructive story of the life of our most common thrush presented in authentic color with delightful narration.

"The Wood Thrush." 10 min., color, sound, rental $3.50, shipping charge 50 cents. Excellent scenes of the nesting, hatching, caring for, and feeding of the young of this bird are shown here. The clear, natural thrush songs are a special treat.

BIRD MIGRATION

"Bird Migration." 11 min., color, sound, rental $3.50, shipping charge 50 cents. Here is a good introductory story covering the seasonal habits of migratory and nonmigratory birds. There are animated map drawings of migratory routes and excellent scenes of birds in their natural habitats.

BIRD NESTS

"Bird Nesting Time." 10 min., color, sound, shipping charge $1. The nesting activities and some unusual bits of behavior of thirteen North American birds are presented.

BIRD SANCTUARIES

"Birds of the Prairie." 10 min., color, sound, shipping charge $1. This film demonstrates that in addition to being extremely interesting in themselves, birds should be guarded as an important part of our American heritage.

CURIOSITIES OF THE BIRD WORLD

"The Loon's Necklace." 11 min., color, sound, rental $3.50, shipping charge 50 cents. The Indian legend of how the loon received his distinguishing neckband is told here.

FISH MIGRATION

"The Invader." 11 min., color, sound, rental $3.50, shipping charge 50 cents. The inevitable conflict arising from the demands of a highly mechanized civilization is depicted in relation to the life cycle of the salmon. Described in the film are the main problems threatening their existence—the building of huge dams along the rivers used by the fish, the pollution of the waters by industrial plants, inadequate sewage disposal in cities.

"King of the River." 11 min., color, sound, rental $3.50, shipping charge 50 cents. A companion film to "The Invader." One of Nature's most remarkable life cycles is reflected in this exciting visual story of the salmon. Development of this king of the river from spawn to full growth makes a fascinating film record. Solid masses of fish leaping waterfalls as they move upstream are doubly impressive in slow motion.

BUTTERFLIES

"Monarch Butterfly Story." 11 min., color, sound, rental $3.50, shipping charge 50 cents. Wonderful close-ups portraying the life cycle of the monarch butterfly. The film clearly shows the four stages of growth— egg, larva, chrysalis, and imago.

SEAGOING MAMMALS

"Seal Island." 27 min., color, sound, rental $10, shipping charge 50 cents. Scenes of the life of the seal colony which inhabits the rocky shores of the Pribilof Islands in the Bering Sea in May and June each year.

WILD MAMMALS

"Squeak, the Squirrel." 11 min., color, sound, rental $3.50, shipping charge 50 cents. This illustrates how an animal can learn to find food that is hidden from view or out of reach. Aside from showing how Squeak learns, the film points up the value of the scientific method of investigating animal behavior.

REPTILES

"Snakes Are Interesting." 11 min., color, sound, rental $3.50, shipping charge 50 cents. Here is a good introduction to understanding this maligned member of the reptile family, with close-ups of many harmless snakes, and also several poisonous ones. It includes scenes of the birth of snakes showing both egg-laying and live birth.

RECORDINGS FROM NATURE

The following unbreakable vinylite records can be ordered through the Service Department, National Audubon Society, 1130 Fifth Avenue, New York 28, New York. For additional information about these records and catalogues of other recordings write to the Society.

BIRD SONGS

"American Bird Songs (Volume I)." 12-inch, 33⅓ r.p.m., $7.75. Some of our most familiar birds are heard on this record, which provides an enjoyable introduction to the birds of America. Also included are game birds, Southern birds, and birds of the fields and prairies, offering the songs of sixty birds in all.

"American Bird Songs (Volume II)." 12-inch, 33⅓ r.p.m., $7.75. A companion record to "American Bird Songs (Volume I)." There are fifty-one bird songs on this record, representing the voices of some familiar birds of gardens, shade trees, and the roadside, little-known songs of some North American warblers, and voices of marsh and water birds.

"Florida Bird Songs." 10-inch, 78 r.p.m., $2.50. The songs of ten birds were recorded in the Everglades. Five of them are familiar; five are the voices of rare or strange birds for which Florida is famous. Especially exciting is the cry of the ivory-billed woodpecker, the rarest bird in North America.

"Western Bird Songs." Introduction and identification by Arthur A. Allen. 10-inch, 78 r.p.m., $2.50. Ten songbirds familiar to bird lovers in the western part of North America are included here.

"The Mockingbird Sings." 10-inch, 78 r.p.m., $2.50. Two particularly talented mockingbirds are featured on this record. The first bird sings the song characteristic of its species; the second gives a glorious medley of songs and snatches of songs mimicking more than thirty other species.

SONGS OF FROGS AND TOADS

"Voices of the Night." 12-inch, 33⅓ r.p.m., $6.75. The record captures the distinctive trills, croaks, calls, and songs of thirty-four species of frogs, toads, and tree frogs in the United States and Canada.

About the Author

DONALD CULROSS PEATTIE was born in 1898—on Midsummer's Day which, he claims, is the best birthday in the calendar because it's the longest day. Being born in the city (Chicago) helped to make him a naturalist because the lack of wild nature there made him beg his parents to be sent to the country, where he could hear loons and owls, waterfalls, and wind in the balsams.

For a while Mr. Peattie was in the publishing business in New York, but he soon went back to college to train himself in the natural sciences, and was graduated with honors from Harvard in 1922. He worked for a while as a botanist in the Department of Agriculture in Washington, and then began his career as a nature writer, with a newspaper column.

When he was 24 he married a girl whom he had met in high school, Louise Redfield Peattie, the novelist. His first nature book, *An Almanac for Moderns,* received the Gold Medal of the Limited Editions Club, and this was followed by *Singing in the Wilderness* (about John and Lucy Audubon), *Green Laurels* (the lives of the great naturalists), *A Prairie Grove* (about pioneer days in the Middle West), *Flowering Earth* (about plant life), and *The Road of a Naturalist* (an autobiography). With Noel Peattie, the youngest of his three sons, then aged sixteen, Donald Peattie wrote *A Cup of Sky.*

Mr. Peattie was a Roving Editor of *Reader's Digest,* and until his death in November, 1964, he traveled often and widely over America and Europe to gather materials for articles on nature and history.

About the Artist

RUDOLF FREUND was born in Philadelphia, Pennsylvania, and attended both the School of Industrial Art and the Academy of Fine Arts in that city. It was after spending two years with the Grenfell Mission in Labrador—in 1936–1937—that he produced his first nature illustrations. Today he is recognized as a master in this field. He has done a vast amount of work for *Life,* including many of the feature illustrations for "The World We Live In," and has illustrated many books, among the latest of which are *The Desert Year* and *Great American Nature Writing,* both by Joseph Wood Krutch. He lives on a farm in East Haddam, Connecticut, with his wife and three young children.